THE GUNSMITHS HANDBOOK

MUST-HAVE SKILLS FOR SUCCESS IN THE FIREARMS INDUSTRY

DANE WEATHERSTINE

The Gunsmiths Handbook
Must-Have Skills for Success in the Firearms Industry

Print ISBN: 979-8-35095-247-6
eBook ISBN: 979-8-35095-248-3

Materials and other works have been prepared by or on behalf of Dane Weatherstine
for general informational and educational purposes only. The author makes
no representations or warranties as to the completeness or accuracy of the
information. In no event will the author be liable for any errors or omissions
in the information contained in this work. The author does not assume any
responsibility for the use or misuse of information contained in this work.

Technical data presented here, particularly technical data on the handloading and
on firearms adjustment and alteration, inevitably reflects individual experience with
particular equipment and components under specific circumstances. Such data
presentations therefore should be used for guidance only and with caution. The author,
Dane Weatherstine, accepts no responsibility for results obtained using this data.

ABOUT THE AUTHOR

The Author of this book, Dane Weatherstine, was born and raised in Baltimore Md. He was not raised around firearms because his mother had always been anti-gun and his father was not in the picture. His mother held on to this irrational fear that a firearm will kill someone because in Baltimore, killings were a daily occurrence. It took many years for her to understand that this was not the fault of the firearm but rather the person and possibly a mental health issue in some cases. Nevertheless, the home remained gun free.

After high school and a number of jobs, Dane stepped into an Army recruiter's office and made the decision to join the Infantry and fight in Iraq. He was sent to Fort Benning for OSUT (One Station Unit Training) where he was first introduced to the M4 rifle and later the M249 SAW (Squad Automatic Weapon). It was on Sand Hill that he realized how much he loved working with the M249 machine gun so when he got his first set of orders sending him to what was then Fort Hood Texas, he landed a position as a machine gunner with the 1st Battalion, 8th Calvary Regiment, 2nd Brigade Combat Team. As an active-duty Infantrymen, it did not take long to deploy into Iraq with this new team. Many missions later Dane was medically discharged because of the injuries sustained while fighting there.

Following that, Dane decided to start attending college using the GI Bill to better himself. During this time Dane needed work and it just so happened that an old friend had called to catch up and, in talking, Dane got a job interview at a local range as an RSO (Range Safety Officer). He started work there as a customer advocate and in a few short years became the training manager and lead trainer. He loved working for this company but as luck had it, he also loved a woman who worked with the company named Julia. She was educated and fun to be around so against company policy he asked her out. A few more years later, Dane and Julia were getting married, and it was Julia's turn to serve in the US Army. Life has a way of bringing you back full circle and this was no exception because Julia's first duty station was, in fact, the same Fort Hood Texas Dane had served with many years prior.

Having relocated to Texas in the middle of what was the craziest covid induced shutdown of this country, finding work was very hard. Most places were forced to shut down and the places that could stay open were well staffed for that same reason. Dane started firing off his resume and a few odd jobs later he found himself working at another gun range. Texas had labeled gun ranges as essential businesses and were allowed to continue operations during Covid. It was at this new gun range Dane became a state licensed firearms instructor, NRA and USCCA instructor, and completed his Associates in Firearms Technology with the Sonoran Desert Institute. After many years of watching people struggle to solve their firearms related problems, Dane decided to author this book.

CONTENTS

INTRODUCTION TO BASIC & ADVANCED GUNSMITHING

This book was written to instruct people of all skills and abilities in the basic knowledge to own and operate a successful gunsmithing business. Having said this, simply knowing the things listed throughout this book will not guarantee that you will be able to start a business and do well. It takes years of dedication and hard work to build a new business into a successful one. My name is Dane Weatherstine and I have taken two different existing shooting sports businesses and turned them into successful Federal Firearms Licenses. This is where I learned the ins and outs of the firearms business and why I feel the need to share this with you today.

Please note that firearms laws change constantly and that I discuss things like the requirements to apply for your own Federal Firearms License throughout the book. At the time of publication this type of information was up to date with ATF regulations but some of these may have changed by the time you read this so if you plan on starting your own Federal Firearms License than please check current ATF regulations on what is required.

A quick note to those with years of firearms experience under their belts already. You can't know what you don't know until it is shown to you. What I mean by this is simply that there are a ton of things you still do not know because you have never had to deal with them or even contemplate them up to this point. I do not claim to be the expert at this and mention my school and classmate's multiple times throughout this book because the knowledge I collected while getting certified as a gunsmith is the same that I am giving to you today. I had no idea how much I did not know until I was face to face with the issues I discussed in this book.

For those of you with business experience but not a ton of knowledge about firearms, this book takes a look at both. Please note that a lot of what you are going to learn as a gunsmith will come from firsthand experience so do not be shy about offering your services even if it is a firearm, you are unfamiliar with. Simply let the owner of the firearm know that this firearm is new to you and that if they are okay with it taking an added moment, you would like to look up the necessary information before starting any work. The customer usually appreciates the honesty and will likely give you all the time you need to do the job correctly.

Finally, trying to diagnose an issue with a firearm that you cannot physically handle is incredibly difficult because there could be ten different reasons for the one issue the customer is experiencing. By using one of the methods I use in this book, you may be able to narrow down the issue enough to tell the customer one of the top three reasons they are experiencing the issue. Knowing exactly what is wrong will require a hands-on approach that may include a test fire and possibly some coaching for the shooter to resolve the issue completely.

SECTION ONE: THE FIREARMS BUSINESS

Costly decisions for the beginner gunsmith.

While looking to price out some equipment, I did what most people do today, and I looked everything up on Amazon.com. One of the main reasons I did this was because this site uses ecommerce to source items from a variety of places and I knew I could find a good range of items to choose from. In doing so I found a large price gap between the equipment that may work and the equipment that will definitely work. Some of the simpler equipment like the spindle/grinder polisher and the tumblers have a relatively smaller price gap of about $100 with the grinder ranging from $50–$150 and the tumblers ranging from $90–$250. However, when we begin to talk about the difference in price between the basic and more advanced belt/disc sanding combo and the sandblasting cabinets the price gap becomes 10 to 20 times more for the nicer equipment. With a belt/disc sanding combo you can spend anywhere from $100 to a whopping $1,600 for all the bells and whistles. The sandblasting cabinets range from $200–$2,000 with size and blasting guns being the biggest difference in cost.

With Regard to purchasing the polishing equipment, I would recommend spending the money on nicer equipment. Because the price difference is not that much, and the higher end equipment seems to have drastically better reviews from others who have purchased it, I would recommend springing for the top end stuff. More than likely, you will use this piece of equipment a lot and having something with the power needed for those tough jobs and the durability to last a long time means more work completed and more revenue generated. It took me a long time to find out that if you buy cheap then you will more likely buy twice. In addition to the spindle/ grinder and polisher you will need a few other items to achieve the desired result. For example, a number of spindle sewn cotton buffing wheels are needed because once you add a specific compound to the cotton you should not add other compounds to the same wheel. This can result in a mashup of compounds that may do the opposite of what you needed done because the different compounds represent a different abrasiveness and mixing them will give you an unknown result. Online you can find a package deal of six different compound bars in 40oz sizes with each yielding a different result. It is recommended you begin with the more course compound and move toward using the finer compounds at finish for the best results. These compounds are easy to use in the bar form in conjunction with the bench style polishers. Just turn on the wheels and while running lightly press the bar type compound on the spinning cotton wheel. You should see the white cotton wheel turn the color of the compound you are using. This means it has plenty on it and is ready to start using.

National requirements for a business to obtain firearms licenses.

The national requirements for a business to obtain firearms licenses include several important steps. To start the individual applying for an FFL must be at least 21 years of age. The person also cannot be prohibited from possessing a firearm. Finally, don't lie or fail to disclose any information on your forms and have a location where you plan to operate your firearms business out of that meets the needs of the FFL. In other words, do you have the means to secure your firearms, and do you understand the requirements for a firearms sale or transfer?

The requirements for obtaining a firearms license in your state, county, and city are similar but with a few differences depending on the location you plan on opening your firearms business. For example, if the city or county you are opening in does not allow the manufacture of firearms in their local area then you would be prohibited from that specific licensing. It is important that the individual applying to the ATF for an FFL send a copy of their application to local law enforcement for approval and notification purposes. The future business cannot conduct business until local law enforcement and the ATF have reviewed the application and have inspected the potential location for a means to secure firearms on the property. If the individual applying for an FFL gets approved by the ATF for the FFL, then the business has 30 days to comply with local law enforcement requirements before opening the doors for business.

Business licenses and permits that are required to open/start up a firearms business in my area.

So, to conduct research and find out what business licenses and permits are required to open/start up a firearms business in my state/location I will need to look up business licenses and permits for Killeen Texas which is considered Bell County Texas. In doing so I jumped on Texas.Gov and found a PDF on just this and found what I needed starting on page 65. This section covers guns, firearms and shooting ranges and list the forms, permits and environmental regulations that must be met in order to start a firearms business in my area. Specifically, it provides me with links to the Texas DPS site to get a firearms instructor license, a link to the ATF Licensing and permits page where I can find more information on what is needed for the federal firearms license, and multiple links to Industrial and Hazardous Waste Regulations so I can meet the environmental standards needed for a live fire facility.

Taking from my past experience working at and managing firearms businesses, I too would open a limited liability company that has a federal firearms license and a live fire facility that is open to the public for general recreation. This can be a huge undertaking if you are starting from scratch and learning things as you go. Luckily, I have a number of years' experience running firearms facilities from around the country with two very different business models to begin creating my own.

In managing different facilities, I took notes on everything from what is expected from a customer advocate to the legal requirements necessary to operate legally and efficiently. I have worked with teams of twelve to make an already popular facility even more so and I have run facilities with a total staff of 4 to make a dying company Known and profitable again. Having worked on both sides of the fence I have learned that every business needs to account for change and be ready to pivot a business model to tailor the needs of the community and continue operating at its peak efficiency.

Regulations regarding trading firearms for a firearms business.

Living here in Texas, if one individual wants to trade with another individual you can do so with little to no paperwork involved. Though a bill of sale would be smart, so both individuals have a record of who has their old firearm, to the best of my recollection it is not required. Now in my home state of Maryland it was required that you and the other individual make an appointment with a state police officer who will record the firearms serial number and will then transfer the firearm from one person to the next. Maryland also had a cool off period of 7 days so even though we took the necessary steps, the state police still informed us that the transfer of the firearm would still have to wait a week. It is important to know your state's laws regarding firearms transfers in general to avoid issues.

As a business with an FFL the "trading" of a firearm is as simple as having the individual fill out an acquisitions form with their information and taking a copy of their ID. Then the firearm is put on your FFL records as a firearm that is ready for disposition (sale). Then the individual who traded in their old firearm for a new one will then complete a 4473 to complete the process of acquiring their new firearm from the FFL. As the FFL a few things are important here. Have two records for this individual for the "Trade." One is filed in the acquisitions book as the source of the firearm that is now for sale, and one is for the disposition of the firearm they traded for via 4473. Finally, it is good practice to check the worth of the firearm the individual is wanting to trade for before the paperwork and "trade" are complete. You would not want to check after just to find out that this was a deal that the FFL lost money on.

The requirements for importing the firearms your business wants to import.

What firearms would your business import?

If I were to go through the trouble of importing firearms then I am going to look for either a large surplus of firearms for cheap so I can increase my profits and build an inventory, or I would be looking for the incredibly rare items that do not jump my inventory by much but should hold healthy profits. In my experience, gun shops follow one of a few business models and that can be either a volume of cheaper sales or fewer firearms of real quality that hold value. Both usually cost a bit to achieve but in this aspect of business I feel it is important to know the people you're selling to. If they like volume, then stock up but if they like quality then do your homework and cherry pick only the best.

The requirements for importing the firearms your business wants to import.

In order to start importing firearms I would need to make sure that my FFL is either a type 08 or type 11 and if importing anything other than sporting shotguns, ammunition for these types of shotguns or parts for sporting shotguns, then I would also need to be registered with the ATF in accordance with the AECA or Arms Export Control Act. As an individual with an FFL type 08 or type 11 I can only import firearms once I "obtain an approved ATF F 5330.3A (Form 6, Part I)"allowing me to do so and once I begin importing them they "must be marked in accordance with the provisions of 18 U.S.C. § 923(I) and 27 CFR § 478.92."A failure to do so may result in legal trouble and the firearms will not pass through customs.

The firearms your business should sell and the services you should offer as a live fire facility.

Explaining the specifics of one type of firearms business.

I believe it is important that you have a live fire facility for a number of reasons. First off, I am a licensed instructor for Texas LTC, the NRA and the USCCA and all three usually require a course of fire to be completed. Secondly, with the number of law enforcement agencies and security officers who hold level III certifications around me currently, having a place for them to train and qualify lands contracts that help pay the bills. Finally, because I offer both lessons and gunsmithing services, when the client's firearm fails to function correctly on the range, I become their immediate first stop for help.

Firearms your business should sell & why.

With regard to the firearms your business should sell, I feel like it is important to both build a brand and search for other well-known brands to sell as well. Everyone knows what a Glock is because of their reliable product line and their well branded name but can those same people tell me anything about

SAR USA? I intend to offer custom built firearms to the customers specs while also covering a wide range of brand name and off brand firearms. Having something for the holster of every customer's price point ensures that I get sales from both the super-rich and the middle-class individuals who want to protect their loved ones while also being able to afford to feed them.

The services your new firearms business should offer.

As I stated before, being a gunsmith with an FFL who sells firearms on location at a live fire facility that offers classes is my business plan, becomes it comes full circle and covers all the bases.

Most have a specific focus on either the guns or the range but being all of those things can help ensure a successful business. When gun sales are down across the country, the training side of the house does well and vice versa. Aim for one tiny target and you may miss it but by using the shotgun approach I'm bound to keep getting hits day in and day out.

One Specific Type of Firearms Business and Who your Customers Should Be.

As I have managed two different Gun Ranges in the past, I believe this is the type of firearms business you should attempt to start. This means you will need an FFL to buy, sell, rent, gunsmith, and manufacture firearms. If I were to describe the layout of the basic facility, it would have two different shooting bays to handle a large customer base and to allow courses to be run while also having a space for walk-ins to shoot. I would keep a minimum of two classrooms to rotate classes out of, a space dedicated to all the equipment needed to be an effective gunsmith and a lobby to display and sell firearms.

Having a facility that meets those requirements brings in a wide range of customers. From the ones who are applying for their license to carry and need a course from a certified instructor to the others who just want to shoot to have some fun, these types of facilities become a one stop shop for just about anyone. Including things like gunsmithing and custom firearms builds is almost a necessity as you can catch customers having issues with their firearm and recommend certain repairs, upgraded pats or maybe just a new firearm in general right there on the spot. Individuals with shops designed specifically for gunsmithing may not have a ton of local competition depending on the region but if the gun range the customer is shooting at has a gunsmith on staff the customer never needs to look for a gunsmith in the first place because it got taken care of already.

Your competitors & what may distinguish your firearms business from others.

Your competitors from a national perspective?

Now that firearms sales can be conducted online and shipped from my FFL to another for the end user, literally everyone everywhere is a competitor for firearms sales. Sites like Gunbroker.com even allow individual owners to sell their firearms online with the promise to follow the law with respect to the legal transfer through an FFL. Even so, as a business who sells firearms in a market like that, it would be smart to offer online sales, if possible, even if you do just get the occasional sale.

My competitors from a local perspective and what you need to consider.

Locally, because I lived in Texas at the time of publication, my competition will range for several reasons. There are a number of gunsmiths around Texas but that is their main focus. Toss a stick and you will find another gun store that sells the same firearms you do. Ever tried competing with a Pawn Shop price, it is impossible. I could put a focus on the manufacturing of firearms but then I have big name companies who call this place their home too. Finally, we look at the Gun Range side of it all and realize that anyone with some land and a dirt berm can call it a range and become competition. That is why being a gunsmith with an FFL who sells firearms on location at a live fire facility that offers classes is a good business plan, becomes it comes full circle and covers all the bases.

What will distinguish your firearms business from others around your location?

My FFL would have an edge being a live fire facility because we can rent the facility to NRA and USCCA instructors. This would not only bring repeat business but also ammo and firearm sales. We can test fire firearms we are buying used to ensure we are not purchasing junk guns at a premium price then turning around and unknowingly selling a broken firearm. People can trust that a used firearm through my FFL is in good working order. People may just come to shoot and realize that their firearm is not working and ask for our gunsmithing service. Even better, they will realize they are a terrible shot and ask if we offer courses. By having everything the average shooter might need in one place you double or triple your business with multiple individuals because they do not need to look for the service, it's immediately available to them at my location.

Resources your firearms business would need to appraise firearms.

The way I have always gone about giving someone a price on a firearm, whether one is being bought or sold, is to use the Blue Book of Gun Values. This is a widely known reliable source for firearms of any type. From antiques to the more modern firearms of today, this service has almost everything you are looking for. The Blue Book of Gun Values also makes finding your exact make and model pretty easy. Just type in who makes it and subcategories pop up (Pistol, Revolver, Rifle) for that manufacturer. Once you have narrowed this down and found the make and model of the firearm, this service will show you every variation of that firearm and how much it is worth in today's market based on things like the current or last listed MSRP and by checking out the sales history of the firearm. If the demand for a particular firearm has dropped in recent years, then you can expect the price of the firearm to drop as well. If the quality of the firearms finishes or function is poor, then this too can diminish the firearms value and The Blue Book of Gun Values will help you determine the worth of the firearm accordingly. Finally, this service usually lists any factory altercations to the firearm that may add or subtract value such as the manufactures specialty grips or the optic that came with the firearm.

With regard to what firearms my business will be appraising, the best answer is probably any firearm that the individual owner wants done. While it is true that firearms worth less than $1,000 do not need an appraisal for insurance reasons, it still may be smart to have one done for every firearm to get a greater sense of what your total collection may be worth. On top of that you may think your old beat-up firearm is not worth anything and find out it is rare and worth thousands of dollars.

As I have worked for a number of different FFLs over the years, I can say firsthand that appraisals are important for many reasons. First and foremost, one of the industry standards for firearms appraisals is to use a BlueBookofGunValues.com subscription or literature and it will become your first source every time you need a price. This site will show you the firearms' last or current MSRP pricing, different listings for the value of the firearm depending on the quality it is in, and even show you historically what it was worth in the past. Showing a history of the pricing helps me determine if the firearm is increasing, decreasing, or flatlining in value. Knowing how much I can re-sell a firearm for and whether that will change in the future has an impact on how much I would offer to purchase someone's firearm.

When someone comes into the gun range and would like to buy, sell, or trade a firearm and there is a question of what the firearm is worth, my first step is to look it up in the blue book of gun values. Showing the firearms worth to the customer usually eliminates a lot of the back-and-forth price gouging and lets them know that you are being as fair as you can as a business who relies on profits to continue operations. I would absolutely go to a Gun Store, Range, Pawn Shop, or any other establishment that uses the blue book of gun values for firearms appraisals because that usually means they are not in the business of ripping people off. If the establishment does not use the blue book of gun values to determine their appraisal amount, then I would be looking for different certifications to determine the persons knowledge of firearms and pricing and maybe research the books they are reading their pricing out of. At the very least I would be sure the pricing they are reading in the book was from the current year as the market for gun values may vary wildly depending on the make and model.

Considering Specifically What the Firearms Market is like in My Location and what to consider in yours.

Continuing with this line of thinking and considering specifically what the market is like in my location is a little tougher than picking three marketing ideas in general. I am located about ten miles from a large Army base here in Texas. This means we have a general population that is comprised of a large majority of soldiers that need to be able to shoot. That sounds great, especially for a live fire facility but it has its drawbacks as well. Soldiers being stationed here may be here for a few years at best before moving on to another duty station or getting out entirely. Landing a customer doesn't always mean a customer for life even if you provide the best services and have the best facilities. This also means that the same marketing techniques that worked before may not work on a new portion of the population that has just arrived.

On the other hand, we have a decent sized portion of the local population who is retired and still love to go shooting for recreation. These individuals are beyond their years of golf and contact sports and find pleasure in shooting. Working a senior discount into the daily range rate may initially mean less income but knowing that some of these people live on a strict budget and making it readily affordable means more visits to the facility.

At any rate or age, I will run into one major issue with my location here in Texas and that is everyone's ability to just shoot on their own properties. Usually when the weather gets nicer the indoor gun ranges here in Texas see a decrease in foot traffic for this exact reason. The public sees this type of business as necessary and to make this point, I would like to point out that during the Covid epidemic when a lot of local businesses were forced to shut down, Texas labeled shooting ranges as essential businesses, and they were able to push on.

My top three approaches for finding customers and why I have selected these.

When looking for a new or fresh customer pool for your business there are tons of things you can do to try and increase foot traffic. The three I would like to focus on include the use of social media for networking, your websites existing marketing tools for advertising, and forming alliances with other local businesses in the shooting sports field and offering services in return for customers.

Most of us already use social media as a networking tool in our own personal lives and have a good idea already as to how it works. Creating social media accounts for your business with your contact information or business location is a good start because the person who finds your social media account but has no way to contact you will likely move on to another person for the work they need done. And of course, nowadays you can pay the social media sites a sum of money to advertise your business to your specified target audience.

Next, we have your website and its existing marketing tools for advertising. Speaking from experience, work on an easy to navigate site that is both informative and useful to the consumer before you start marketing it and your business. Jumping into advertising and getting people to navigate to your businesses website that is under construction or just one page with little to no real content is a quick way to have your potential customers ignore you in the future. Once your site is in good working order then start looking into the marketing tools it offers. By adding things like a subscriber sign up you may begin to land people who have an interest, and you can begin using email marketing campaigns and weekly newsletters to be sure your business stays in their thoughts, and they come to you for business.

Finally, creating a relationship with other businesses in your area can be difficult, especially if they offer some of the same goods and services as you do. Introducing yourself and your business to local companies can open a line of communication and this could result in more business or at least a better insight to your local shooting sports market. If you specialize in restoration work and another local company keeps a focus on newer custom build type work, then when they have a customer asking for restoration work, they will reference you and if you get someone looking for a custom build you can reference them. Working together like this means better business relationships and more happy customers who found exactly what they needed.

The demand for firearms in my location, how this matches the ones I would sell, and what you should consider.

What do you believe the demand might be for firearms in your location, and does this match the types of firearms your firearms business would sell?

Here in Texas, there will always be a demand for firearms. Once the state changed its laws last year making Texas a permit less carry state, sales for smaller, easy to conceal handguns went up. Usually around the different hunting seasons you will also see a rise in specific sales such as shotguns when it's time to bird hunt and bolt action rifle during deer season. My firearms business will sell every type of firearm, but you may see the inventory fluctuate throughout the year to meet the need of the public.

Do you foresee this demand remaining steady, or will it fluctuate?

Demand will always fluctuate with regard to firearms sales and what is selling. News hits that you won't be able to buy an AR-15, and everyone runs out to get one. Election season rolls around, and you may believe new more restrictive gun laws will be passed so you purchase the firearms you want while you still have the chance. Riots are moving closer and closer to your neighborhood, and you want to be able to protect your family. The demand remains steady because this is a dangerous world we live in and having the most effective tool to protect your loved ones or put food on your table means the difference between a confident person and a victim.

Your firearms business may need to sell a variety of different types of firearms to meet customer demand.

Yes, your firearms business will need to sell a variety of firearms to meet the customers' wants and needs. Texas is an open carry state so not every carry pistol being sold has to be small and concealable. Come different hunting seasons the demand for different types of rifles and shotguns is needed. And finally, what I like to shoot may not always be the customers preference. What might feel good in my hand may feel like junk in yours because of things like hand size and personal preference.

Elements necessary to effectively manage a firearms business.

As someone who has had the opportunity to manage two different firearms facilities for years at a time, there are several things you must get right to help you manage effectively and get your business growing. To start, you must keep your books tight. This means it is necessary to train and re-train your staff on the paperwork side of the house. Always getting a second set of eyes on the paperwork usually allows you to catch any mistakes. Depending on location and volume of gun sales, the ATF will absolutely do audits so do not slack on your bookkeeping. Next, I would have to say a hardworking, trustable staff is key to success. I have had to let people go in the past for theft of cash, ammunition and even firearms so be sure you can trust your staff before allowing them to handle cash or firearms unattended. This work can have a lot of fun moments but don't let that fool you because managing a facility can be a lot of work too. Keeping training schedules for contracts, multiple instructors, and staff training while also gunsmithing, being a customer advocate and being the one to teach a bunch of the courses can stretch you thin. Let us not forget ordering and inventory because without these your store front will be empty and that equals lost revenue. It takes good customer relations to know what is selling and what is not, so keep your thumb on the pulse of your customer base so you're not buying things you want but rather you're ordering the things that continuously sell out. Dead inventory as a new business can equal a dying company.

Managing a firearms business during a national tragedy, or after a mass shooting incident.

Managing a firearms business during a time such as the scenario described.

Unfortunately, mass shootings are a reality. Some of which never get spoken of and others tossed all over the news turning what was in fact a tragedy into a national tragedy. Allowing your customers to ask their questions and finding ways to answer them is all just part of the business. Usually, it is better to stick to facts and leave one's opinion out of it to avoid any confrontation, especially on the hot button issues. Nevertheless, you have a business to run and, in my experience, when things like mass shootings happen, gun sales go up. I have yet to meet a person who wants to be the victim in a situation like this and usually when things like this hit close to home, everyone begins looking for the best tool they can find to defend themselves and often that is a firearm.

As a firearms business manager, responding to customers who are angry or upset when they represent both sides of the gun control debate can be part of the job.

Check your politics at the door ladies and gentlemen. Usually, no one will go to the gun range looking for a fight and because the business I am managing has a live fire facility, Angry or upset customers from any side of any debate may be denied the right to use the range if the staff have determined they were not in the right state of mind to shoot. Flared emotions have no place in a facility designed for recreational shooting and on numerous occasions in the past we have denied peoples range privilege for this reason alone.

As a firearms business manager, dealing with angry customers who come into your place of business with the sole intent of purchasing firearms to seek revenge may happen.

I have personally had to deal with a number of customers in the past where during conversation they have said a number of things that prompted me, the seller, to halt the gun sale. Things like "I'm going to head downtown and start wasting drug dealers" and "Wait till I see "Blank" again, I got something for him" have been said to which I had to inform the customer that I could go no further in their gun sale. This will likely take an angry person and send them into a rage with a new focus on you so if you do not do well with confrontation then best to grab someone who is.

Managing a firearms business and maintaining your composure and emotional responses or reactions is important. Your opinions shape the way you operate your business.

It is best to approach people with a friendly helpful demeanor when running or managing a firearms business. As we have already said, have your customers check their politics and emotions at the door if they intend to do business. Staying neutral keeps you from offending some or insulting others. Often if you allow a customer to trip your emotions it can escalate certain situations into something it did not need to be. The goal is to calm the person to a point where you can get them to leave with minimal confrontation. People have a tendency to mimic each other's emotions and if you approach the situation calmly and remain calm throughout, the upset individual will likely begin to relax.

Challenges you may see when setting up your own shooting sports business.

The business structure you choose if you were starting your own shooting sports business is important and can make or break a new business.

If you were to start your own shooting sports business, you should form an LLC or limited liability company. This allows you to shape the company in a sole proprietor fashion without the liabilities falling directly on you like with having just a sole proprietorship.

The challenges you may see when setting up your own shooting sports business.

Usually, one of the biggest hurdles someone has when starting a shooting sports business that has a range for live fire activities is the startup cost. Using companies like Action Target makes the actual setup process easy but costs a ton of your initial startup capital. However, you can opt to build the range yourself if you're good with a welder and know the basic setup of this type of facility. Having worked with two different facilities, both taking these different approaches, I can say that building the range yourself saves a ton of startup costs and gives you the ability to make the range operation as simple or complex as you like. Action Target systems are complex and use computers and microchips that read exact distances and can-do things like timed drills with turning targets but with this technology comes problems that cost even more money to repair or replace. Rigging a simple motor to a pully setup and welding the carrier boxes yourself is as simple as it gets and though you sacrifice the ability to do some of the cool things, repairs are cheap, and you have a better understanding of the systems having built them yourself.

The challenges you may see when managing a shooting sports business.

Managing a shooting sports facility has its own set of challenges. Once a facility becomes popular and you get more and more contracts and customers, the business has a lot of moving parts. Managing my current facility here in Texas feels like home and though the business grows year over year, it still has not reached the scale of the facility I managed back in Maryland. My old facility ran at an almost 24/7 capacity with police contracts in the early mornings, a wide customer base during the day and security contracts running shoot quals late night into the early hours of the morning. If you start a shooting sports business that becomes popular, then staffing becomes a challenge. It's relatively easy to manage a small facility with little staff and limited hours but running one that operates 24/7 becomes difficult.

Creating a shop "Standard Operating Procedure" for a general machine/gunsmith shop.

Personal safety—First and foremost, everyone is responsible for safety. If you or anyone sees an unsafe act, you are entitled to address it with the individual or shop management. Regarding your own personal safety, we require that you wear the proper personal protective equipment and follow all guidelines for safety considerations on or near any of our machine equipment.

Machine training—We would like to see all our staff cross-trained on equipment, so everyone has at least a general understanding of how it works. Please do not attempt to use any of the equipment in this facility without the proper training and supervision first. For you to use a specific machine on your own you must demonstrate to management a proficiency on it first and be certified.

Holding and adjustments—While holding or adjusting any item or machine being worked with in this facility it is important to take the proper safety measures to ensure that you or those around you avoid serious bodily injury. Machine adjustments specifically should be done while the machine is off, and power is pulled. This is to ensure that you do not damage the machine in any way and that the machine cannot accidentally be turned on during your adjustment.

Moving material—There are a number of different materials in this shop that can be hazardous to your health. These can come in the form of a solid or a liquid and should be handled with the proper safety equipment while transporting. If you are injured while moving any materials in this facility, please see management immediately so they can get you the first aid needed to address the injury.

Shop layout—Please take the time to learn our shop layout. Because of the volume of business we do, and the number of staff we have, it is important to know who and what is around you at all points in time. You may see the same piece of equipment in multiple areas of the shop. This means it has a specific purpose to that area and should be used as intended. If you need a piece of equipment that is not in our facility, please notify management and we will do our best to get you what you need to complete the job appropriately.

Lighting—it is important that you can see what you are doing as you are doing it. Every area of the shop should have adequate lighting but in some cases the machine you are using has its own light source to better see the object being worked. If at any point you cannot see what you are doing because of poor lighting, please notify shop management and they will work to remedy the situation as soon as possible.

Cleanliness—We do expect some areas of the shop to get dirty as things are being worked on. The buildup of this type of mess can be dangerous and can cause damage to the item being worked. Please do your best to clean up any mess left behind before moving on to another area of the shop. Keeping up with the overall cleanliness of the shop is everyone's responsibility and is important to the success of the business.

Dust and chip collection—Some machines in this shop will create an abundance of dust, debris and metal flakes or chips. It is important that the user uses the proper personal protective equipment while operating machines that do this. It is also important that the individual making this type of mess in the shop clean their workstation before moving on to the next. It may take more time to finish the item being worked on because of this but it is vital to the cleanliness and overall success of this business and will be managed by every employee working in this facility.

Ethical concerns that are important to consider each time you receive a firearm for gunsmithing.

Identifying one case of unprofessional work that has been performed on a 1911, how this work negatively affected the operation of the firearm and information as to how this work should have been performed for a better outcome.

I found it hard to locate a lot of unprofessional work done to the 1911 platform. Not to say there isn't a ton of it out there, but most people will not advertise poor quality work to the world. I was able to find an illustration on thearmorylife.com titled *"don't do these things to your 1911"*. The source is a blog of sorts put together by Springfield Armory and can be considered credible because this company makes a number of 1911 models and would never recommend something unsafe. In the illustration you see someone who has used rubber bands to disable their grip safety. This negatively impacts both the safe operation of the firearm and the user's ability to control the firearm because it allows the user to fire with an incorrect grip.

Deactivating a safety is never advised and can lead to legal trouble if the firearm is accidently discharged and someone is injured or killed. If you dislike the way the grip safety feels or are having trouble activating it while firing, you can look at an aftermarket grip safety that feels better and is easier to activate. A lot of 1911 grip safeties have a flat palm type grip safety and if this is hard to use correctly, I would recommend something that has an added bump at the palm section of the safety. This raised bump makes it easier to activate even if the shooter doesn't have a perfect grip. I have been asked by customers in the past about this and I usually recommend this raised type grip safety because it is a quick parts swap and is next to impossible to mess up or damage the firearm.

The most valuable resources you have available to ensure that you return a firearm to your customer in better condition than you received it.

As a gunsmith some of the most valuable resources available to you are your cleaning tools. Most of the time when a customer hands you a firearm that needs work, they are handing over something that was just fired or has been carried for an extended period of time without cleaning. One of the easiest ways to return a firearm to a customer in better condition than when it was dropped off is just to disassemble it and clean it up. Not only have you fixed their problem but by handing back a clean firearm the customer knows you took good care of it.

Ethical concerns are important to consider each time you receive a firearm for gunsmith work.

It is ethical to return any old used parts of the firearm that were removed or replaced. I have known one or two gunsmiths in the past to keep any parts they removed and replaced stating things like "well they don't need it anymore because they have the new part installed." I usually return these things to the customer and let them know that the old parts are with the order and if they say something like "just toss it" then I may end up keeping the old part so long as it is not broken. Returning the old parts that are still serviceable allows the user to reinstall the original factory parts if they later decide they don't like the new upgrades.

A firearms business owner needs to be more concerned about record keeping NOT less.

Record keeping as a business is always a smart thing to do. Whether it is invoices for orders of firearms accessories or actual firearms sales, it helps to keep track of what is coming and going and what profits were being made. Well-kept books make it easy to look something up if you need to know the cost or even where you purchased something specific. Keeping separate record books for both your firearm sales and other inventory will make it even easier to locate the paperwork you need.

For inventory other than firearms you just need one record book for the invoices of the product being ordered but for firearms it's smart to keep multiple. Some of the most important records a firearms business would need to maintain are those of the firearms Acquisitions and Dispositions. As a firearms business you will need inventory and that is going to come from other FFL's. Keeping a detailed acquisitions record book allows you to keep track of the dealer transfers and keep up to date FFL information on file. More importantly, having a well-kept up to date disposition book for all of the 4473's from firearms sales can make or break your FFL.

On occasion you may be contacted by the ATF looking to do a contact trace. This means they need a copy of your 4473 as proof the firearm was indeed sold to the person of interest. Also, as an FFL you are subject to audits where ATF agents will need access to all of your records so they can be sure you are doing what is required by law. A few mistakes can be expected, and they will notify you of the ones they find but missing records and a ton of issues and you may end up losing you FFL all together.

The important components of an operating budget a firearms business must have for success.

Your startup budget is vastly different from an operating budget for one main reason. Usually most of the startup cost for opening a business is a one-time investment. This means that it may cost a lot more, but you will not have to pay for these things annually or on a regular basis, like with an operating budget. When considering what your operating budget may end up being you may want to look at things like water, gas, and energy consumption. These will be paid on a monthly basis like your rent or mortgage so figure out what that is going to run on average Fand include it in the operating budget. Also, staffing can play a huge factor in your operating budget. Starting small and being the only employee to complete the days tasks can save money but as the business grows you will need a staff so consider how many people you may need, how much you can afford to pay them and at what frequency they will be paid and include this into your operating budget as well.

Next, we have your inventory to consider. The money made on these products does not become all profit because doing so means you did not restock as inventory was depleted. Start seeing the products on your shelf as how much markup or profit they make and not the MSRP because you will need to take a good portion of the initial cost of the product and reinvest in future orders to stay stocked. For example, this magazine cost me $10 from a distributor and I am selling it for $14.99 as MSRP suggests staying competitive with other businesses. I should not take the $14.99 made to pay an employee, I should be taking the profit of $4.99 for payroll and use the other $10 to purchase another magazine to sell.

Finally, we have repair cost to consider in an operating budget especially considering my business model includes a live fire facility. Anything down range will get hit with a bullet at some point. Lines, trolleys or carriers, security cameras etc. all will get destroyed with time and a down lane is lost revenue. Consider charging a specific rate for damages if a customer has cost you money in repairs so this issue kind of pays for itself.

Tax considerations a firearms business must prepare for in general, most people do not think about the taxes they charge and what additional charges for which they should prepare. The tax on sales in your business is subject to the state tax you are opening shop in, but did you consider if the county you want to open up in has a separate tax amount they expect. A brief example of this could be that the state you open up in wants you to charge 6% tax on every item sold but you had no idea the county you opened up in wants an additional 0.5% tax on the same items. This means that if you sold $10,000 worth of inventory then at 6% you collected an additional $600 in taxes that should be paid to the state quarterly if you are smart. But wait, you should have charged 6.5% tax to cover the counties tax expectation as well. This only ends up being an additional $50 but if ignored for long enough becomes a lot more and could be the reason your business fails or loses its license to operate. No one likes paying taxes but if you do not keep your numbers tight than the tax man will be paying a visit for sure, so charge your customers the necessary taxes, pay what you owe and move on.

Important bookkeeping a firearms business owner and business manager must know.

In order to summarize the important bookkeeping basics a business owner and business manager needs to know for running a firearms business you will need to break it down into a few different sections of work. An example of this would be what paperwork is firearm related and what paperwork is not. Breaking down the firearm side of the paperwork, you will need separate books for your acquisitions and dispositions. That just means where you got the firearms and a list of the FFL information and a detailed record book of where the firearms went or who purchased them. I may also be smart to keep separate acquisitions books for what was a dealer transfer for a customer who bought the firearm online and are having it transferred to you and what firearms came directly from a manufacturer or distributor.

Now, the other side of your paperwork is not as important as how detailed your firearms paperwork is required to be, but it is still important to manage these things as well. A business usually has more cost than just the inventory that is ordered and sold. An easy example of this could be entering your business and seeing that a few lights don't turn on. This may only be a few dollars for new bulbs, but it could be something more serious and require that you hire an electrician to fix the issue. In any case you need to keep your receipts and invoices in order. Maybe the electrician will warranty their work and a month later the issue will be back. Do you know who did the work and exactly when they completed it? Did you save the invoice with the warranty information on it? If not, you may end up spending even more to fix the same issue.

An important note here is that there is a difference between bookkeeping and record keeping. While the recordkeeping that has been discussed is vital to the long-term success of any FFL, the bookkeeping specifically refers to the financial records of the business. The businesses sales, quarterly taxes, payroll, and operations cost such as repairs or office supplies all play a factor in a well-rounded business model. When looking at a business's budget, forgetting some of these factors can land you in some hot water. I think I have $2,000 to make orders and blow it later to find out that I now need a few hundred dollars for operational cost which can leave me with down equipment until the sales of the order start to return the needed funds for repairs. While it will always be important to mind the big stuff, it is sometimes equally as important to remember the little things.

Employee training for a firearms business is important.

Product Knowledge: How you should train your employees to know the ins and outs of the firearms your business is selling.

Training employees on the firearms that are being sold and their functions is an important part of the sales aspect in a firearm-related business. If a customer has a question about a particular firearm and your answer is "I have no clue" then they are a lot less likely to purchase it from you. We encourage employees to handle any firearm being sold or rented for range use so they have a good working knowledge of the product and can pass that on to what is hopefully the end user. It is even possible that we could train staff in new firearms before they are being sold so on day one the staff are knowledgeable and can help push sales.

Hiring and Training New Employees: How you plan to hire and train new employees, to be prepared to work in the firearms business.

This is a tough business to get into and often companies only hire those who can show an abundance of knowledge and certifications or those who they already know and trust. Regarding the training offered, I would say it depends on the job they are being hired for. If they are customer advocates responsible for sales then training on the point of sale, 4473 process, and the inventory would be key. If they are being hired as firearms instructors, then they should come with a solid base of knowledge and certifications but would need to demonstrate the ability to pass that knowledge to the student. If the new employee is going to be listed as a responsible person on the FFL, then it's all training focused on fast bound and the proper filing and storage of critical paperwork. No staff members will go untrained, and all staff will continue their training regularly as things change constantly.

Evaluating Employees: How you evaluate the employees, especially with regards to their performance in the business handling firearms and working with customers.

One of the first things a staff member of mine will be evaluated on is safety both on and off the range. If the hired instructor can't be safe on the range, then it is time for more training to ensure they continue safe practices. If they continue to be unsafe after that then it's time to let them go. If a customer advocate doesn't do something correct on a sale or the 4473 process, then once again it is time for more training but if it continues then it may be time to demote or remove them as well. You can be a great salesperson but if your paperwork is consistently incorrect then I run the risk of losing my FFL after an ATF audit. Staff should always have an opportunity to correct their mistakes but depending on their position, you must draw the line somewhere.

Ongoing Continuing Education: How you develop plans for continuing education of your employees, along with your own continuing education.

When developing a plan to continue education for both the staff and me, it may help to have outside experts' step in to help. You can't just become an NRA training counselor; you must seek training from the experts and work your way to the goal. Looking to bring in companies like Sig Sauer or Glock for their armors courses gets the staff certified and ensures they are receiving the best source for the knowledge.

A quick breakdown of some of the most important things a firearms business needs to consider.

I will summarize a few of the topics and discuss how I would approach it and what may or may not be required. To start let us talk about the Firearms Customer. If all your business does is firearms sales, then the market has some serious booms and busts. However, opening a gun range along with my FFL to sell and manufacture firearms I keep those customers coming back.

When predicting customer demand, it can be important to remember a few things. Do your customers hunt and what season is approaching? What type of firearms should be used for the animals being hunted? These things would affect what I'm ordering and when. If you live in a city, then you may need to find a different type of customer in your local market. In this case I would look at what new firearms are hitting the market and what demand there may or may not be for them.

Let's not forget the ever-important gun laws and legislation required to open a firearms business. They can be broken down from federal to state and even county laws and it is important to keep current with them as in some areas this changes regularly. Obtain your Federal Firearms License with the ATF and don't forget that when you submit your paperwork to them, you will also need to send a copy to your local law enforcement for review and approval as well. Then there are the general business licenses and permits to consider. Getting a tax ID number and possible EIN numbers for W2 employees is important and the business is required to display their sales and use tax permit at all times.

Finally, creating a sustaining business structure that continues getting people in the door and spending money is make or break for a new firearms business. Having product, the customer will continuously need ammunition, and this may equal returning customers. But don't forget that one of the best, cheapest, and easiest ways to retain your customers is to remain friendly and helpful every time someone visits your location. If the customer doesn't feel welcome and leaves unhappy, they are not likely to return to your business.

Key principles of federal law applicable to firearms transactions.

To start you will need to determine if the person attempting to purchase a firearm is eligible. This means they are not a prohibited person. Next, you need to determine if the person buying the firearm is going to be the actual owner or if they are going to re sell it for profit. If so, the individual is "engaging in business" and technically needs an FFL to do so. You will also need to know this because they may be attempting a straw purchase for someone who is prohibited. Finally, if the person doesn't have an active carry license for the state they are purchasing in then a "NICS" check or background check must be done again to determine that they are eligible to continue the buying process.

The National Firearms Act

The national firearms act is a deeper dive kind of background check if you will. Someone attempting to purchase things like machine guns, destructive devices or short barrel rifles will need to fill out additional forms and submit their fingerprints to the ATF. NFA items require the potential owner to pay for a tax stamp or "Transfer Tax" which can vary in price. Something like a suppressor requires a $200 tax stamp but Any Other Weapons (AOW's) only require a $5 tax stamp. However, if the transfer is between two FFL holders, then the "Transfer Tax" is not required.

The Concept of a Prohibited Person

A person may fall into the category of a prohibited person for several reasons. This may include things like being a fugitive, being convicted of a crime that is punishable for more than one year in jail, being an unlawful user of illegal drugs, being committed into a mental institution, being an illegal alien, having a dishonorable discharge from any branch of the armed forces, renouncing your citizenship, having a restraining order, being convicted of domestic violence, and a few more things. It is important to note that a person indicted for a crime that is punishable for more than one year in jail may continue to own firearms purchased prior to the inditement. It is also possible that someone who doesn't fall into any of these categories can still be prohibited. For example, as an individual selling a firearm you have the right to refuse the sale for something that was said during the transaction that leads you to believe the individual doing the purchase intends to do something illegal like assault or murder. A prohibited person could also be someone who intends to purchase a firearm for someone who can't legally own one. This is called a straw purchase and is a crime.

SECTION TWO: GUNSMITHING BASIC KNOWLEDGE

The purpose of a test fire when working with firearms.

There may be many reasons for a test fire on a firearm. The first being the customer claims something is not working correctly with their firearm. In this case you may need to test fire to see the actual malfunction they were talking about in order to better understand the issue and find the best way to resolve it. In other cases, a test fire may be part of ensuring a firearm you built yourself actually functions. With an FFL that allows the manufacturing of firearms you can purchase all the parts you want for a build and assemble the firearm from scratch. This, however, means that you should test fire before selling the firearm to ensure the product being put out for sale is a functioning one.

As someone who has spent a number of years working for live fire facilities, I have seen countless firearms I was unfamiliar with and was then asked to clean, diagnose, or fire them. This can be a little unsettling at times especially when it is a much older firearm worth a fair bit of money. In such cases I would usually admit to the customer that I am new to this make or model and that it would take me some time to do the research to complete the task the correct way. Doing research is one of the best ways to make an unfamiliar firearm safe to test fire. The firearm may be in great working order but if you the operator have no idea how it works it may yield unsafe results. Now if the customer is ok with someone who just admitted to knowing little about their firearm to complete the task, then do as you promised and take the time to do it right. At the very least, if you did make a mistake then you don't look like someone claiming to be a professional but having no clue.

The first thing you must know before attempting to disassemble or inspect a firearm.

The first things I need to know about a firearm before attempting to disassemble it is who makes it, is it loaded and how does the safety work. Knowing the make and model points me in the right direction and takes some guess work out. Knowing if it is loaded or not is important for safety and knowing if the firearms have a safety and how it works goes with that. After that it would be important to figure out how the make and model is broken down, even if just for a quick field strip for cleaning. Most Handguns have a takedown lever located above the trigger and trigger guard, but this will change from brand to brand and model to model. A fair number of rifles use machine screws that need to be removed before disassembly and most shotguns require the use of a punch to remove pins for a breakdown. No matter what the firearm, step one is safety and step two is learning the method in which to begin your disassembly.

Bluing and Browning, both hot and cold methods.

Both cold bluing with Perma Blue solution and Browning using Laurel Mountain solution give you the fastest results and do not require the user to heat the metals to work. If you cannot afford an expensive setup and do not have days to get the work done, then these options may be the best choice. This is not to say they yield the best results or that they do not require a lot of work to be done right. It is only to say that they get results faster than the other methods. Laurel Mountain solution is to be applied every three hours and can get satisfactory results in about four coats depending on the finish you desire. Cold bluing can be applied to the surface every few minutes and can get satisfactory results in 6-8 coats. Both require some surface preparation that can be done with a few pieces of fine grit sandpaper. You will also need an applicator swab or cotton ball used to apply the solution and they require steel wool to re-prep the surface in between coatings. Other than that, no real equipment is needed to perform the task. These chemicals can be dangerous if inhaled or if they get on your skin so be sure to use gloves when applying and be sure you are in a well-ventilated area.

Hot bluing and your basic browning do require some equipment to get the job done right and you will need specific chemicals to achieve the desired results. When hot bluing it helps to have the right tanks that utilize burners underneath. This gives the user comfort in knowing they are getting an even heat throughout. I have seen people use tanks on bricks and a single burner underneath and this usually will not yield consistent results if just the middle of the tank reaches the correct temperature. When rust bluing or "Browning" firearms the process seems safer in terms of the fumes let off like when hot bluing. Simply apply your browning solution directly on the parts and hang them in a damp box. This is needed to speed up the rusting process required to achieve the desired finish. Once a light coating of surface rust develops remove it from the damp box and boil the parts in distilled water for about 20 minutes. This helps turn that red rust into a black surface coating. Clean it up with a wire brush or some steel wool (free of oil) and repeat the process about 7-8 times for the best results. Both hot bluing and browning can off gas some pretty bad stuff so please be sure that when attempting either process you are in a well-ventilated area and wearing the proper personal protective equipment like gloves and a respirator. If you want a deep black finish to the firearm, I recommend browning the parts because when hot bluing with Nitrate bluing salts you will get a blue tint in the finish.

Do you believe you will be able to complete the detail-strip of your firearm?

I would be able to detail strip the Glock pistol completely because I have all of the tools and training needed to do so safely and correctly. There are still a ton of firearms I would not be able to say this about because it would be impossible to know every step for every firearm that walks through the door at the range I currently work out of. On top of that, some firearms have firearm specific tools needed in order to completely break them down and I do not own those tools yet because I have not been faced with those issues yet.

Having the Glock Armorer Certification helps me with regard to the knowledge and confidence needed to fully disassemble and inspect Glock firearms. Before I took this training course, I had never broken a Glock all the way down because I was not sure what I was looking at and I was afraid I might break something. Sitting with a certified instructor who walked me through the steps helped me build confidence and since then I have no idea how many Glock pistols I have worked on. My advice is to seek qualified instructors and training as often as possible and become a well-rounded gunsmith.

Attempting to troubleshoot a customer's weapon without being able to fix the parts.

Though I believe it is necessary to be able to fix fasteners and other small parts, I also believe it is reasonable to begin the trouble shooting process even if you are unable to fix the part causing the problem. Step one is always clearing the firearm and if the customer was claiming it will not chamber a round and you find out it was because they were loading them backwards, then the problem is solved. You did not need the ability to fix small parts to solve this problem. Most of the time you will not have the small part that has broken on hand anyway so why not begin the process to at least identify the issue component. Now if the part in question is not fully broken and you are able to fix the part to get the firearm working again then awesome, but you will never get to that point in the process until you make the attempt. Recently I was given a 1911 with a removable front sight. The client was getting older and wanted Tru Glow sights to be put on so he could see it better. This is usually a few minutes of work with double that going into making sure they are lined up correctly. However, the front sight I was provided was not made for that make and model firearm. It was my ability to use files correctly to reshape the sight to fit that allowed me to see the job to completion. However, there is no shame in turning down work because you are not comfortable attempting something you're uncomfortable or unconfident with. I did it for years before I had the confidence to try more stuff.

The differences between standard and metric measurement systems.

Some differences between the metric system and the standard system are their units of measurement. For example, regarding length the metric system uses millimeters, centimeters, and meters while the standard system uses inches, feet, and yards. When talking about the difference between units of measurement regarding mass the metric system uses kilograms and grams while the standard uses pounds and ounces. Some might argue that one is better than the other, but most people are not taught both and present biased opinions.

I believe the metric system is the preferred method of measurement across the world today because that's what is being taught to everyone since birth in most regions. We didn't grow up in the time when these decisions were being made and we could contribute to the outcome of these decisions. Instead, everyone is taught from grade school one unit of measure or the other and almost never get taught both. So, when you think metric is the standard, then it gets taught to the next generation and so on. I don't think one is preferred over the other, I just think people are taught one OR the other and that becomes THEIR standard.

Finally, I do not believe the US should adopt the metric system because as this week's article reads, doing so now would be considered a "time-consuming and expensive hassle of changing the country's entire infrastructure." The US has a hard enough time with its current infrastructure and deciding to switch from standard to metric would just be way too expensive, not to mention confusing to most people who were never taught it. What are your thoughts on this?

The troubleshooting process and focusing on the common elements.

To start with I believe everyone should focus on safety as it applies to every interaction someone should have with a firearm. This could mean anything from determining if a firearm is safe to shoot by using a bore scope and looking for damage, to the actual function of the firearms safety selector options. A focus on safety keeps everyone out of harm's way so always start with that.

The next is a pretty simple one. Does the firearm feed ammunition and how exactly? This is going to change wildly as firearms over time have changed so much. The firearm can use anything from a blind box magazine that is internal to the firearm to the cylindrical magazine the Calico pistols used in their development. No matter what magazine type the firearm uses, focusing on its feeding operation can be critical to the firearm's proper operation.

The following I would group together as it is the multiple steps that follow whenever a trigger is pulled. The Firing, Unlocking, Extracting and

Ejecting are critical to the firearms operation but can be identified with some quick research of the make and model in question. Once these things happen it is a matter of whether or not the firearm re-cocked its firing mechanism in the process. If the hammer does not reset or it refuses to cock, then it's time to open the firearm up and start looking at parts. I had one customer with the Pawn Shop Special Glock that would not fire. Turns out it was missing its firing pin entirely so be careful of what you buy and from whom you buy it.

Practicing a guided investigation of malfunctions using multiple different firearms.

To properly make a firearm safe, these are a few checks you could perform.

Making sure the firearm stays pointed in a safe direction. Remove the firearms feeding source. Open the action and inspect for ammunition. If the firearm has a safety selector switch, make sure it is in the safe position before moving on.

In the Browning Auto 5 long recoil platform, at what point in the movement of the action parts is the spent case ejected and where is the ejector located?

Now this is an interesting firearm. This shotgun has a barrel that recoils with the bolt after the shot. Once all the way to the rear the two extractors hold the rim and as the barrel travels forward without the bolt because of its recoil spring. It then releases one of the spring-loaded extractors and the pressure on one side of the rim coupled with a barrel that is now out of the way equals ejection of the spent case. The extractors also work as ejectors and there are two of them, one on each side of the bolt.

In the Glock short recoil system, what components unlock the slide and barrel from one another and when does this happen?

The recoil and the pressure of the round being fired kick the slide back and in that moment the barrel tilts and drops out of battery. This unlocks the barrel from the slide allowing for extraction and ejection.

In the inertia recoil system, what component is responsible for driving the bolt assembly rearward and how does this component receive its energy to do so?

The locking head has a recoil spring behind it and they both sit inside the bolt itself. The inertia of a fired round pushes back on the locking head and compresses the spring that stores energy that now wants to push the bolt back for extraction and ejecting.

When analyzing the locking phase in the recoil system and comparing it to that of the blowback system, what do you notice?

The blowback system does not store energy and begins the extraction process immediately. The locking phase in other recoil systems allows for a split-second delay in the extraction process and stores the energy before allowing it to release and cycle the firearm.

Tests and checks that I would perform on a revolver prior to returning it.

Yes, two of the most important things I would check are the cylinder stop and the spacing between the cylinder and barrel mouth. A few Taurus Judge revolvers I have seen do not catch on the cylinder stop and if the cylinder moves just past the catch and the firing pin is struck with the cylinder out of alignment it may result in damage and injury. Likewise, if the distance between the cylinder and barrel mouth is too great, the round exiting the cylinder and entering the barrel mouth may catch a little resulting in metal flake and burning powder escaping and being blown outward and this can be dangerous.

Common methods for clearing the feed source for single & double action revolvers.

The feed source on both single and double action revolvers is the cylinder that locks into the frame. Clearing the double action revolvers usually is as simple as pushing or pulling the cylinder release button and using your other hand push the cylinder out of the frame. After physically and visually inspecting for the presence of ammunition, if ammo is present, keep the firearm pointed in a safe direction, tip the muzzle up and press down on the ejector bar connected to the cylinder and swing arm. This should drop any rounds out of their chambers but remember to double check. With a single action revolver, you can remove the cylinder, but this may not be the best way to clear the firearm and is usually done to clean the cylinder. Keeping the firearm pointed in a safe direction quarter or half cock the hammer and open the loading gate located on the side of the frame. Then turn the cylinder until you have inspected each chamber for ammunition. If a round is present in one of the chambers, use the ejector rod located just under the barrel and a spring-loaded rod will push the round out one at a time.

Single action only revolvers & the visual clues you have with this type of action.

A single action only type revolver is one that cannot be fired unless the hammer is manually cocked. Usually, the visual cue would be how the firearm is loaded. Single action revolvers can open or be loaded a few different ways with the standard being the side loading gate. Another way would be the breach load where the frame opens and swivels forward. You don't typically see single actions with a cylinder release like on the double action.

In general, there are less connection points in a single action revolver which means fewer moving parts to function. In most cases the trigger links directly to the ledges on the hammer when double action revolvers use additional parts. Also, in some cases but not all, a single action revolver uses a metal bar as a trigger spring when actual springs are used in most double action revolvers.

Double action only revolver & the visual clues you have with this type of action.

A double action only type revolver is one that cannot be fired in single action mode. This means there is no external hammer that can be manually cocked prior to pulling the trigger. Some double action only revolvers have an external hammer that has had the hammer spur removed and others keep all of the components internal, and a hammer cannot be seen.

In general, there are less connection points in a single action revolver which means fewer moving parts to function. In most cases the trigger links directly to the ledges on the hammer when double action revolvers use additional parts. Also, in some cases but not all, a single action revolver uses a metal bar as a trigger spring when actual springs are used in most double action revolvers.

The differences between troubleshooting a single-action and a double-action revolver.

I believe this is still going to depend on the make and model of firearm on which you are working. For example, with most single action revolvers the cylinder will not move until you quarter or half cock the hammer but with the Ruger Black Hawk single action revolver once the loading gate is opened the cylinder will rotate even though the hammer is all the way forward. On occasion I will get shooters with new Heritage Rough Rider single action revolvers that tell me it will not fire. This falls into the operator error category because often times single and double action revolvers do not have a safety selector, but Heritage Rough Rider single action revolvers have one located on the opposite side of the loading gate that prevents the hammer from coming in contact with the firing pin.

A select few double action revolvers have an internal safety that requires a specific key to lock and unlock the hammer. If a customer tells me the revolver is locked up and will not cock or fire this is one of the first things I look for. Sometimes double action revolvers will not allow the cylinder to close and lock and this is usually because the ejector rod has unscrewed to the point where it is too long and prevents the cylinder from closing. I will also have customers asking me how to open the cylinder on a single action revolver to load it. When I explain how to load it through the loading gate they are confused because double action revolvers have the cylinder drop out of the frame to load. This only begins to scratch the surface of the issues customers will ask you to trouble shoot with regards to single and double action revolvers, but these are some of the most common I have come across.

Transfer bars and what they do in a properly functioning firearm.

The transfer bar is a type of internal safety that sits between the hammer and firing pin. When the trigger is pulled the hammer will cock while the transfer bar is raised in place to allow the energy of a falling hammer to transfer to the firing pin so it may strike the primer and fire the ammunition. When de-cocking the hammer and keeping the firearm pointed in a safe direction pulling but then releasing the trigger you allow a controlled drop of the hammer, and the transfer bar will drop out of place so if the hammer slips it will not contact the firing pin.

"Cylinder Gap" & the potential negative safety and functionality implications it has.

Cylinder gap is the term used for the distance between the end of the cylinder and the start of the barrel. These should have relatively tight tolerances to avoid malfunction, damage, and injury. Malfunction can occur if the gap is too large and lead bullets are being fired. The soft metal passing through this gap can shave off the bullet and lodge into this gap preventing your cylinder from rotating the next shot. This can damage the firearm but more importantly the pressures pushing through the same gap may expel dangerous debris such as this metal flake and still burning gunpowder.

It may be important for you to understand the development of the modern cartridge.

I believe it is important to understand the development of the modern cartridge because you never know what caliber firearm you will be working on or how the cartridge is fired. Knowing how the priming compound is ignited in conjunction with the way the cartridge is struck may be vital to understanding the basic operation of the firearm you are working on and may solve an issue.

Knowing how the cartridge is made and fired will help the person using or repairing the firearm better understand what may be going on with the gun. At the very least, reading the headstamp on the cartridge will ensure that you are loading the correct ammunition when test firing a firearm. This little bit of knowledge has helped me a lot regarding my work as an RSO at a live fire facility. Too many times I have seen people try to load the wrong caliber into their firearms and it will either jam because the ammunition is too large, or it will lock up the action because the smaller caliber expanded and cracked the casing in the bore of the barrel. When someone asks for help on the range because their firearm is not cycling correctly, I will often check the type and caliber of the ammunition they are using first.

Modern cartridges and their operation can be the difference between safe usage and catastrophic failure. Trying to fire a .300 AAC Blackout through a barrel chambered in 5.56x45mm often results in a seized up and cracked bolt carrier group, a swollen upper receiver, and everything blowing out through the baseplate of your magazine. .300AAC Blackout and 5.56x45mm use an almost identical rim and case dimension but the .300AAC Blackout is too large of a projectile to push through a 5.56x45mm barrel and so once the primer is struck and the gun powder ignites the pressure looks for the fastest escape and if you're lucky that is through the magazine. Knowing the similarities in case size and the dangers involved in using the wrong cartridge would make me more cautious when handling the firearm and its ammunition.

How steel types and machining processes have changed in the past 50 years.

Depending on the type of steel used to make the firearm, the service life of the weapon may vary greatly. Of course, this is still dependent on how the individual owner stores their firearm. Mild steel with low carbon content may be more prone to rust and make a fine finish harder to achieve. Mild steel is often softer than steel made with other alloys included. This softer steel is more malleable and makes creating things like the receiver on a rifle easier to machine. Today we have all types of alloy elements in steel to harden or soften the steel and depending on the part and its function multiple types of steel may be used on one firearm. Alloys added to steel today include Chromium, Cobalt, Manganese, Vanadium, Tungsten, Titanium, Silicon, Phosphorus, Nickel, and Molybdenum. Each serves a different purpose and gives that steel new traits like better density or it may help resist softening at high temperatures. It helps to know the alloy in the steel you are using because

Cobalt decreases the steel's ability to harden while Vanadium increases the steel's ability to harden. This is important if you want to try case hardening because if the steel has that decreased ability to harden then it may not harden or may take a lot longer to get the desired result. Another reason you may want to know what kind of steel you are working with is if you are going to engrave the metal. It may help to have a mild steel when doing this to make the process a little easier.

Manufacturing processes today have enabled gun makers to produce consistent quality firearms through the use of things like the CNC machining process. With this computer program type of machining every piece of metal comes out the same way every time. Making todays gunmakers worry a little less about overworking a part and wasting materials. This newer process means gun makers can produce a lot more products to meet the customers' demands but quality control is still really important. Back in the day when a gun maker would undergo heat treatment of the metal parts, they had hands on every piece but when going from one- or two-guns parts to 1,000 guns parts a day, things can get missed and your quality control begins to slip. It should go without saying that a quality handmade firearm with no stress cracks in the steel is going to last a lot longer than one with poor quality that gets abused more.

The science and definitions of both velocity and speed.

Both velocity and speed are quantities used to describe the motion of something. So, before we define velocity let us talk about something called displacement. Displacement can be defined as the distance (straight line) between the final position and the starting position with the final position being the direction the object is traveling toward. Knowing this, we can say that the average velocity of something can be measured by dividing the displacement of an object by the total time it takes to travel to its final position.

Instantaneous velocity is finding an object's velocity at an exact point of time. Velocity can be measured using an old school technique and a ballistic pendulum. Using a block of wood suspended by two cords you can shoot the block and by measuring the momentum of the blocks movement on impact you can derive the bullets velocity.

Now, finding the speed of something can be done by measuring the distance of an object's travel and dividing that by the time it takes for it to travel that distance. Instantaneous speed is capturing how fast the object is moving in one specific moment in time. Ammunition manufactures and even the at home reloader can measure the speed of a projectile using a chronograph and is usually relayed as FPS or feet per second. In conclusion, the differences between speed and velocity are that speed is a scalar quantity while velocity is a vector of quantity and speed is found by calculating distance divided by time and velocity is found by calculating the displacement of the object divided by time.

The physical science that applies when firing a bullet.

When a cartridge is fired it rapidly accelerates the bullet and as it is being pushed through the barrel and exits the muzzle of the firearm, it is moving at some amazing speeds. This extremely fast-moving projectile does not have a constant velocity because that would mean that it is traveling in a relatively straight line and that no matter how far out you attempt to measure the velocity it would read consistently despite the distance covered or rate of time passed. Without a constant speed and direction, you can determine that the projectile's velocity changes. We now know that there are several things that will affect the projectile's flight so let us cover a few of them right now.

Extreme long-range shooters know this as an unavoidable fact because when we start talking about hitting targets at a mile out, factors like gravity, wind speed, and corellas effect affect that straight line motion. The shooter usually lines up their shot, pulls the trigger and sees the projectile move in a straight line when in reality, gravity, and resistance slow down and drop the bullet back down to the ground. Long range shooters understand this and usually must shoot high of the target to ark the projectile to fight these forces and rain that round onto target. Finally, I read in a textbook that an object projected horizontally, and one dropped vertically should hit the ground at the same time. It may be hard to believe but this concept should work the same when using a bullet that is fired out of a gun vs one that was dropped at the same height as the guns muzzle. Shot perfectly horizontal, the bullet is moving fast and covers a lot of ground quickly but will inevitably fall to the ground at some point. Different distances travelled at very different speeds, but the one dropped and is falling due to the constant rate of gravity it is experiencing. This was eye opening to me for sure.

The concept of chemistry relates to gunpowder and primers.

Without the carful considerations of the different types of chemical reactions as they relate to things like gunpowder and primers, shooting could be either non-existent or extremely dangerous. What I mean by this is that the wrong chemical reaction or even too much of one in the wrong firearm and you may be creating a dangerous situation while adversely a different chemical combination could result in no reaction and no shot at all.

Primers used for small arms today typically need a few things to work and these can include stuff like explosives, fuel, oxidizers, binders, sensitizers and frictionators. Explosives range from TNT to mercury fulminate and are the bang, but something needs to start this reaction. While it is true that TNT is also a sensitizer, we still need things like aluminum powder or ground glass to act as a frictionator to get things to spark our reaction. Finally, like all fire, we need fuel and oxygen, and these can be found in things like gum Arabic which doubles as both a fuel and a binding agent. When used correctly and in the right amounts the chemical reaction, converting from a solid to a gas, will ignite the gunpowder that creates hot high-pressure gas used to launch projectiles through the barrel of a firearm.

The chemical energy it takes to move that bullet through the barrel has to be substantial and because there are so many different calibers used today, the firearms internal ballistics need to be considered. So, let's find a few examples of what I am talking about. Let us say that we replace primers and gunpowder with baking soda and vinegar, do you really think that will push a .50BMG down a barrel? Probably not. What about a Squib load (primer pushes bullet partially down the barrel but not out)? The lack of explosive could not create enough chemical energy to push the bullet out and you either realize this and rod out the bullet or you don't and cause damage and injury to yourself or others. In conclusion, the right combination of elements is vital to the chemical energy needed to get a firearm to function as intended and this chemistry changes wildly in today's market.

Factors I would consider before recommending a specific material for barrels.

Assuming I am working at a firearms manufacturing facility, the materials used for barrel construction will vary depending on many factors. I would begin by figuring out what caliber firearm this will be. Knowing this may limit what materials can and cannot be used for the job. For example, a 22LR might fit down the barrel of a 223 but the material used for the 223 barrels may be considered overkill, costly or even too heavy for a 22LR firearm. Next, I need to know if the barrel will need to be machined to attach the front sight directly to the barrel. Certain alloys and treatments machine well and cut easily but others will take more time and attention to get this done correctly. The tougher metals could also cause my tools and bits to wear faster as well.

It may help me to know how much abuse the barrel will be taking regarding how many rounds it can fire and at what rate they will be fired. It may also help to know what environments it can be used in. If the intended barrel is for the larger caliber precision shooter, you may want a 416R Stainless Steel barrel. This type of barrel works well for the precision shooter and yields great results but if used in temperatures less than 0 degrees Fahrenheit the barrel may fail. A Chromoly Steel barrel on a firearm meant to be a machine gun would be a good idea to drastically increase the barrels life and help it stand up the abuse. Also, chrome lined barrels are most often hammer forged which makes them exceptionally durable compared to other methods. I have burnt out a few barrels because they were never intended to be used as full autos. In any case, a real conversation should be had with your client to determine exactly what their best option would be moving forward with barrel construction.

The forming processes, attributes, and the treatments used by Glock.

The brand of firearm I have chosen to discuss is Glock. The quality controls Glock manufacturing uses would be hard to beat. Where some companies cut costs by using inferior metals for things like their slides, Glock only uses high quality steel that is inspected by their metallurgical department. An example of a company who cut costs and used an inferior metal is Walther. The P22 model firearm has a recuring issue of having the slide crack so we did some digging. Because of its smaller caliber the company thought they could use cheap pot metal for their slides. What they thought would save them money in fact ended up costing them more because of the number of warranties and repairs they deal with due to this cheap metal. When Glock purchases the raw materials used for their firearms, they will not accept materials that do not meet the standards set forth by their company. In other words, even the raw materials are inspected before they can be used for production.

Glocks polymer reduces weight while promising durability, corrosion resistance and easy maintenance. Their polygonal barrel was designed to provide exceptional performance and a better "bullet-to-barrel fit." Glock also uses advanced surface treatments, and they compare its durability to that of diamonds (though not quite as durable). Finally, Glocks magazine construction uses an internal metal frame with a durable polymer coating to ensure that the magazine is corrosion resistant and remains durable if dropped during use or training.

Glock does everything from tool making to machining every part themselves in-house Instead of outsourcing cheaper parts to reduce costs and increase profits. Glock hammer forges, mills, turns, stamps, and performs their own injection molds themselves. Each department is responsible for each component, and they follow strict quality management and environmental management standards to ensure that the firearm you purchase is some of the best on the market. Say what you want about Glock firearms but in the end, it is a firearm you can be confident will work when you need it most.

Reflecting on previous machine shop visits and describing personal safety & machine safety violations.

Well even though I do not have a ton of experience in gunsmith machine shops, I did learn a thing or two about using a lathe while going to school for glass blowing. While transitioning from military life back to civilian I used my GI Bill to go to school for glass blowing in Salem New Jersey. I did some art courses, and I did some scientific Glass blowing courses and witnessed a number of safety violations during my time there. Normally this was the student's fault and not the instructors. The only real difference between a lathe used for glass blowing and one used in a machine shop for guns is the material you chuck in and instead of bits used to cut metal we had torches to melt glass. I have seen people in baggy clothes get way to close to the lathe and almost get caught up because of it. Also, because this was a school, the teacher and students would all gather around the machine and ignore the minimal standoff distance to get a better look at what was being done. Another issue I saw a lot was individuals not wearing safety glasses in the workshop. Most were not wearing them because they themselves had not started working yet but the issue becomes their proximity to others who were already working next to them. What some people do not understand is that if cold glass is rapidly heated incorrectly it can shock the glass and send shards of hot glass in every direction. Anytime you enter a machine facility of any kind you should always be sure to follow their safety guidelines and wear the proper safety equipment at all times. This helps to avoid serious injury and or death and is particularly important.

The use of files and rasps.

When to decide whether to use a file or a stone is all dependent on how much material you need to take off. Also, there are things I can do with certain files that I would not be able to achieve with a stone. For example, more recently I was handed a Tisas 1911 with removable iron sights and the customer had bought a Tru Glow front sight to replace the one he had a hard time seeing. What seemed like an easy task became one I had to spend an hour working on.

The front sight this customer had purchased was not meant for this firearm and when I informed the customer of this, they responded with "please just make that one work" despite it not being made for that firearm. The cut on the slide was very small and the front sight had too much material on it to just slide right in, so I used a triangular shaped file because it gave me the correct angle I needed to begin removing material and form the shape I needed. For one or two spots I used the flat file, but the square cut file did me no good and a stone would not have been able to get into this tiny angle. For this job I absolutely needed the right tool for the job and there was no way around it. Yes, I believe you can use a bastard cut file on metal and a smooth cut mill file on wood, it just depends on what you are trying to achieve.

The importance of precision measuring tools.

When building an AR-15 Rifle it is important your barrel is at least sixteen inches in length to meet the requirement. This is when using a tape measurer or ruler may be used for the measurement. However, something that long you would not use calipers or micrometers for because these tools are meant to be used on things much smaller. For example, when drifting sights on and off of a handgun you will need to be sure the new sight sits center on the slide to ensure an accurate shot after installation. A caliper can be used to measure the difference from both sides using its depth rod and you would split the difference until the sight reads the same measurement on both sides. Using the SDI Gunsmithing Tools Lab book issued during the course it says that the "dial indicator is used to measure 'travel' or play." They are referring to the tools ability to measure both high and low spots on an item or more specifically when they say play this may refer to the amount of give or movement a machine will read while using this tool to check your mills and or lathes. Another use for the dial indicator is measuring "runout" or the wobble of an item. If using your lathe to machine threads on a barrel, it would be important you know the barrels "runout" at the muzzle you plan to thread.

Describing how I would set up a prep area as if I were going to add finishing procedures to a shop.

When setting up a prep area in my gunsmithing shop I would have a separate area just for prep. This area would not need a ton of space. I would make sure I had enough space to work on more than one firearm at a time but still keep parts from getting mixed up or lost. Prepping the parts in order to add a finish to them may require different processes depending on the type of finish and how it is applied. One of the most important chemicals required for most prep work is a degreaser or a stripping agent. Most finishes do not work well on a part coated in grease or oil so the degreasing agent would probably stay in this part of the shop and more than likely in a solvent tank ready for work. I have known people to use kerosine as a degreasing agent, but this has negative effects on plastic parts and if I am prepping a Glock frame for Cerakote then this would not work well. In any case, chemical strippers and degreasers should not come in contact with skin to avoid the negative health effects associated with it. Things like gloves, eye protection and maybe a respirator should always be used while working with these products. Usually during the prep stage and disassembly I will bag up parts in their specific groups to avoid losing or misplacing parts and to be sure they are free of shop debris. If I have a grinder and polisher in this same prep area, it will throw debris everywhere so bagging the parts is a smart idea. Also, I would try to avoid a ton of shelves and clutter in these areas because if you accidentally throw a tiny spring while breaking down the firearm, this will make it pretty hard to find.

Four visual characteristics that the firearms professional can use to identify a modern finish.

Way back in the day there were only a few methods of conversion coating they could use to finish the firearms, so it was fairly easy to identify what ones were applied to the firearm but today is a different story all together. These days you have Duracoat and Cerakote spray on finishes, Hydro Dip designs that can be laid directly on the parts, different plating, and anodizing type coats and more. The old coatings may still be easy to identify because they won't usually give you different colors or designs like the new ones will.

Some visual characteristics you can use to determine the type of finish used on a particular firearm may vary. If the firearm has a Matte finish, you can determine it may be one of a few types of coatings. Duracote, Cerakote and Anodizing can give you this flat kind of finish and completely cover the bare metal. If the firearm has more of a glossy finish you can determine whether a plating or blued finish has been done. If the coating on the firearm is a design like hunting camouflage it is easy to determine a Hydro dip type coating has been applied. Finally, if the metal has a varying degree of blues, greens and purples and is in an undetermined pattern it is safe to say a that case hardening has been applied to the metal at some point. It is virtually impossible to recreate the exact pattern again and again with case hardening.

In any case, the type of coating you wish to apply to your firearm can vary greatly today. If you want a particular color coating to match your environment, you can go with a spray on finish. Want to blend in with the wood line you are hunting in? Try a woodland camo Hydro Dip in one of many different environment type designs. Got a classic firearm you wish to restore back to its original finish? Determine what was original to the manufacture and it will more than likely require bluing or browning to restore it to its factory finish. Most of the coatings used today protect the bare metal and prevent rust from forming but be sure that whoever you contract to do the work knows what they are doing. It would suck to ask for woodland camo Hydro Dip and receive a distorted wasteland look to the finish.

The differences between laser etched & hand engraved work.

First off, I would want the customer to understand the difference between Hand Engraving and Laser etched type work. Beginning with the tools required to start the work, the laser engraver uses a computer to digitize the image they want engraved and then they will mount the item in place calibrate their cutting laser to the correct frequency needed for the cut desired on the material they wish to have engraved, and they will hit start. This takes some knowledge with regard to the programing needed to digitize the image and the function of the laser engraver itself. However, the skill level stops there because the cutting process really only takes a few minutes and if programed and calibrated correctly the job is done with little to no error. The person who hand engraves the item really only needs a few sharp hand tools and a lot of time to do the cuts with precision.

The cost of a laser engraver can range anywhere from $2,500 to $60,000 depending on its capability and whether it will work on small items or much, much larger items. However, the cost for the person who hand engraves really should not be calculated in the few hundred dollars for hand tools but rather the years of practice needed to get proficient. The operator of a laser engraver can spend a long weekend reading manuals and testing their equipment on scrap metals but the person who hand engraves must be confident in every cut they make, and this doesn't come from a manual.

Now someone using a laser engraver can incorporate vivid detail because the laser used can essentially print/cut it into the surface layer at incredible precision without having to put much more effort into the job. On the other hand, the individual doing hand engraving can do work with a great deal of detail, but this takes a lot of time a patience to achieve and will likely not give the same vivid results as the laser engraver. In other words, if you want detailed work done fast, talk to a local laser engraver. If you want custom hand engraved work with a great deal of detail, allow the time needed for the individual doing the work by hand to achieve it. The trust factor also plays a big role in the work being done. Take the time to do some research and find someone with a reputation for good work. Once something like the family gun has been cut weather by laser or hand tool there is no going back. If the person working with the laser engraver is "new to the machine" ask for some test work first before allowing them to click start. If the person doing the engravings by hand has no other work for you to see, then you are trusting them blindly and again it may be smart to get some test work done first as proof of craftsmanship. Any way you decide to go it will increase the value of the firearm. It may be cost, or it may be sentimental but with the work you want done correctly completed, you will feel like it's the prize piece of your collection.

Two variants of blow back operation type handguns.

For this, I have chosen two rifle length 9mm carbines from different parts of the world. The first is the Windham Weaponry 9mm GMC Carbine made here in the USA and the second is the Israel Weapon Industries (IWI) Model B Carbine made in Israel. While both are iconic in their own ways, they both utilize 9mm semi-automatic blowback operations to cycle while firing. Both also use detachable magazines, utilize a sixteen" barrel with 1 in 10 twists, and have pistol like grips on them. However, the similarities between the two stop there. The IWI Model B Carbine uses an open bolt concept that "improves cooling during periods of continuous fire" while the Windham GMC Carbine uses a closed bolt design. While both do use detachable magazines, the IWI Model B has the user insert the magazine in the pistol grip whereas the Windham GMC has the user insert the magazine in a separate magazine well.

The IWI Model B has a folding stock option while the Windham GMC has a collapsing six position stock option. While both do have sixteen" barrels, the IWI Model B only uses 4 Grooves to achieve its twist rate whereas the Windham GMC has 6 Grooves. The Windham GMC uses billet aluminum for its frame and the IWI Model B uses steel. Finally, the overall length of these firearms does change depending on the stock orientation you choose to run but the IWI Model B still runs three"-6" shorter than the Windham GMC giving it somewhat of a tactical advantage when moving through small spaces during tactical operations. All in all, both of these choices are great options to have but the IWI Model B was only imported by Action Arms from 1983-1989 and can be harder to find with price points that triple. If you are looking for a cheaper option that is readily available than the Windham Weaponry GMC Carbine rifle is your obvious choice.

V springs and the process used to construct them.

At first glance you may not know that a V spring was in fact a spring at all. Most people have this notion in their heads that a spring is that coil of wire with loops on both ends. While this is not incorrect it is also not the only type of spring on the market. A V spring is called that because it is usually shaped this way because of a fold in the metal. A lot of older firearms were made with V springs in the action, but even newer firearms manufacture like Glock Use V springs on the takedown pin to keep upward pressure on the part.

So how are V springs made? First you will need to decide whether you will be using flat stock or high carbon drill rod. Just remember that if you use drill rod you will need to square off the rounded sides. If I am making the V spring to replace a broken one for a specific firearm, then I will need to take measurements of width and length from tip to fold and try to match them with my new V spring. Once I know the distance from tip to fold, I will take a hack saw and cut my fold line about half the depth of the metal bar. Remember to give yourself a little more material than the length of the part you are making. You can always remove it later if need be. Most recommend doing the fold while the metal is hot.

It is important that you check your measurements often during this process. Continuously check things like your width and thickness. To be sure that you have not already removed too much material and are wasting your time. If grinding is needed it should be slow going. If the metal begins to change color, then stop immediately and allow it to cool. Again, if you are re-making a V spring to replace a broken one, everything from the arm to the bend needs to be exactly like the last one so continue to check your measurements.

You may find yourself using flat files to match the taper of the metal arms on the V spring. Do your best to match the exact taper of the old V spring to the new one. And now that we have the required shape and dimensions it's off to polish the part. Tooling marks should be polished away to avoid stress points in the new V spring. Plus, when I go to heat the metal, it may need to be polished for me to see the color of the metal during the tempering process. When heating these parts I will use my high fire Paragon kiln because it is capable of reaching and sustaining the temperatures I need. Once I have fired it to a temp of about 1,400-1,500 degrees and it is glowing cherry red, it is time for my first quench. After a quench it becomes hard but also very brittle so be careful not to break it during this phase.

Off to polish once more and its back into the kiln but this time I will only be heating the metal to about 600-650 degrees. This temperature will vary depending on the type of metal used but most people will get it to about this temperature and its color should range between a dark blue and a gray to know its ready. Do a few final checks on all of your measurements. You should be able to fully compress your new V spring in a vice and once released it should return to the desired measurement. If you are new to this then it is okay if you do not get it on the first try, most do not.

The purpose of a choke and the installation procedure for a ventilated rib.

The purpose of the chock inside the muzzle of a shotgun barrel is to keep the shot that is being fired in the pattern one desires when firing. Some chokes force the shot to group tighter while others may allow for a larger spread on target. Our customer here has requested that a choke be installed that would give him 45% shot charge at 40Yds. That means that about 45% of the BB shot coming out of the firearm lands on target at 40Yds. I believe this to be a wider choke as most would like to see a tighter 70% shot charge at 40Yds. Installing a choke is relatively simple with the right tool. I have seen people try to use flat head screw drivers on one of the notches of the choke to try to loosen it enough to remove it the rest of the way by hand. I would never recommend doing this as you may damage the choke thus affecting the accuracy of the shot being fired. You may also damage the threads that the choke threads into and this means an expensive fix or a new barrel to remedy the issue. Using a choke tool allows the user to catch both of the notches on the choke and with a key like turn it will thread the choke out without damaging the threads the choke screws into.

I have found two ways to attach vented ribs to a shotgun barrel. One attaches to the barrel by using a type of epoxy to bond it to the barrel and the other uses a soft tin/lead solder to create a solid bond and a more permanent bond. If you want to do this job yourself, I advise using the epoxy method because it is less permanent and if done incorrectly you can use a braded fishing line to remove it. The braded line should make its way under the vented rib and separate the epoxy tape Add a Rib uses to attach the new ribbing. If you wanted to solder the new vented rib to the existing barrel, it would require that you first expose the metal where the rib is going to be attached. It is important that you do not grind away too much so you will not need to fix this later on. Place the vented rib you plan to attach to the barrel and mark all the spots where it touches the barrel. Be sure it is lined up correctly before marking the contact points or you may be attaching the rib crooked and need to start from scratch. After exposing the contact points on the barrel add some flux to the contact points on the vented rib, heat it up just enough to apply a little solder and let this cool off. Then place the pre soldered vented rib in place and clamp it down to the barrel again making sure it is not crooked. Apply more heat and flux to the sections that touch, and the flux should pull in the solder and create a solid bond between the vented rib and the barrel. You may need to apply more flux and solder as you go along but be sure not to use so much solder that it protrudes at the contact points.

The rotating bolt operation and one firearm that uses this locking system.

In the gas operated system using a rotating bolt it is the back flow of the gases from the fired round that starts the operation. The AR-15 uses the rotating bolt operation in conjunction with the gas operation. When the gas pushes through the gas tube it reaches the gas port located on the top of the bolt carrier group (BCG) and begins to push it backward. The locking lugs on the bolt face then turn to unlock the bolt from its barrel. The cam pin that sits in a chamber off to the left side of the bolt is sliding out of its channel and into the BCG thus turning the bolt face and unlocking the locking lugs.

Roller, gas & lever delay blowback systems & how they work.

Explaining how the rollers in the roller-delayed blowback system delay the opening of the action.

The rollers in a roller delayed blow-back system works like a locking lug. In the forward position the rollers push into grooves and help to ensure the firearm is in battery before being fired. This delays blowback because it requires a little more pressure to push the rollers in and then allow the slide or bolt to cycle.

Identifying one modern firearm that uses the gas-delayed blowback system and explaining how the gas is used to delay the system.

The Walther CCP 9mm uses the Gas-Delayed blowback system. This system uses a small hole just after the bore of the barrel to allow some gas to escape while pushing the projectile out of the muzzle. The pressure will eventually transfer to the slide for normal operation but this little bit of gas that escapes delay the blowback of the slide. Walther calls this Softcoil instead of recoil.

Levers are usually used to create a mechanical advantage. This is how the levers in the lever-delayed blowback system do just the opposite.

The lever used in the lever-delayed blowback operating firearms creates a mechanical disadvantage. This lever is internal and rotates until it unlocks the bolt or slide allowing freedom of motion for extraction and ejection of the spent casing. The time it takes to unlock or rotate that lever creates the delay.

The SKS uses a tilting breechblock operation. How this works and what are some of its strengths.

The falling/tilting breechblock operation in a gas operated system like the SKS is simpler than it sounds. The breach block that lifts and falls during operation is what is locking and unlocking the bolt allowing it to perform its normal cycle of operation. The piston being driven by a fired round push back on the bolt and the breach block tilts up because it is forced to. Then when returning it falls back into place as intended. One of the biggest benefits this has is a more reliable firearm. Usually if the ammunition has enough pop to throw a bullet, it has enough gas to cycle the bolt.

How the direct gas impingement operation differs from the piston-driven operation.

Both do use the gases from a fired round of ammunition to begin their cycle of operations, however the manner in which that gas is used differs greatly. Direct impingement pushes the gas down a confined tube and pushes the bolt that is in direct contact with it. This method uses the directed gas to push the bolt, separating the gas tube and gas port so the remaining force can be expelled. Piston driven systems use an actual piston to physically move the bolt. The gas traveling into the gas port pushes against the piston head moving the connected rod rearward to physically move the bolt. Both methods work great, but I fall on the fence here. Each was its place in battle but usually the environment where one shines the other perishes. The grass is always greener on the other side.

The difference between dynamic ejectors & fixed ejectors and the pros and cons of each.

A dynamic ejector like the plunger type located on the bolt face is remarkably effective and less prone to malfunction or damage. However, more parts to be manufactured during the building process and more to breakdown and clean. Fixed ejectors are usually one piece of metal located opposite of the ejection port that is fixed in place. This small metal bar can bend or break though and the firearm could begin to malfunction with every shot you take. A benefit to the fixed ejector could just be less moving part and more reliability depending on the make and model. Each serves a purpose, and both work great when properly maintained.

Three similarities and three differences of the Mauser, Straight-Pull, and Mosin-Nagant.

What I think is the most interesting thing about all the rifles we will discuss is their use as weapons of war. Most people hear that term today and automatically think of something like the AR-15(or M4) or the AK-47 (or AK-74) but in fact the Mauser, Mosin-Nagant, and Straight pull type bolt action rifles were some of the original weapons of war because all three were used in WWII. All three also use what is known as "a Cock-On-Open system" and have some type of handle attached to the rifles bolt. However, all three of these weapon systems have some different features as well. For example, the straight pull bolt types sometimes offer a "Cock-On-Close system" as opposed to the "Cock-On-Open system" depending on the model. The Mosin-Nagant rifle type has a bolt head that rotates with the body of the bolt while others have bolt heads that turn automatically to lock when closed. Finally, the Mauser uses an ejector that is separate from the bolt its-self while the straight pull uses "plunger ejectors that are housed in the bolt head".

I believe each rifle type uses different visual cues that help individuals identify the different rifles. However, some of these ques do not always have anything to do with the bolt types themselves. For example, the straight pull is easier to identify because the bolt handle does not rotate to lock and unlock but rather gives the user the ability to just pull the handle straight rearward. Now with both the Mosin-Nagant and Mauser rifles both having rotating bolts, we can begin to look at other features to try to identify them. For example, the Mauser rifle has its rear iron sight mounted by the bolt handle while the Mosin-Nagant has its rear iron sight mounter more forward on the rifle. Also, as long as the rifles stock is standard issue, the Mosin-Nagant rifle has sling mounts in its wood stock while the others use sling mounts that attach to the rifle. All of these rifles have been battle tested and helped to push rifle design and innovation that resulted in the amazing rifles used today.

The "big picture" conclusions you should draw about a client's weapon & it's intended use.

We all know that safety is the goal when dealing with any firearm but when someone brings me a firearm (especially the older ones) the conclusion I need to draw is usually, do they want a pretty gun or a functioning one? This tells me up front what my end goal will be and what is going to make the client happiest. This is not to say a firearm cannot be both but often times it comes down to show piece or work tool. Pretty guns have had lots of care with regard to their appearance but maybe not so much in the function department. Some of the guns I see broken need to get back into a functional state because the client actually uses them to practice regularly and for self-defense. Usually, a carbon filled gun with broken parts tells me they want function because it broke during regular operation of the firearm. If the firearm comes in with rust all over, it tells me they want restoration but probably not function because it had not functioned for years prior and may be beyond a point of safe operation. Safety and function checks are important but differ between the pretty and the working. Maybe for some restorations you need to remove a part used for function to be safe while with work guns you would focus on the actual safety's ability to function. Damage inspections with firearms will differ as well because you may focus on external damage rather than the internal damage that may be the cause of any malfunctions. So, as the question said, regardless of what type of malfunction you are dealing with, if a new customer asks for my help with a firearm the big picture is usually do you want a pretty gun or a functioning one?

SECTION THREE:
BREAKING DOWN THE ISSUES

Discussing the definition of what makes a rifle accurate and what makes it inaccurate.

For this I will reference an article titled "Basic Rifle Accuracy and Ballistics" posted by Terminal Ballistics Research. "If the rifle will be used out to 300 yards or beyond, it will need to be capable of grouping 1" or less at one hundred yards." I agree with the author of this online article because having a large shot group at one hundred yards means an even larger shot group at 300 yards. With regards to hunting, this could result in a bad shot that could wound an animal but maybe not kill it. The author agrees that with larger shot groups "it is unethical to shoot at game."

Later in the article the author begins to describe the definition of an inaccurate rifle by stating "if a rifle produces groups of around 1.5" at one hundred yards, it is unsuitable for 300-yard shooting." Once more I agree with the author and would like to stress how unsafe this could be to try. Any missed shot must land somewhere and if the individual firing becomes too focused on the target and is taking a shot at three hundred yards with a rifle that is unsuitable of hitting accurately, they may miss and hit an unintended target, person, or animal.

What I see a lot in my profession as an NRA instructor and RSO at the range are shooters who buy amazing rifles and scopes with no idea how to use them. The author concludes "that most people are capable of shooting accurately with almost no experience if they are 1) given an accurate rifle and 2) set up appropriately." I can get on board with this statement, however, if I could add to it, I would say that the user should be shown how to use the equipment available to them and be taught some shooting basics. Something as simple as breathing while shooting can ruin a shot at three hundred yards and if someone "with almost no experience" doesn't know this then making that shot safely and accurately becomes increasingly difficult.

The time and expense that goes into accurizing a firearm. Where should someone draw the line?

I tell people constantly that you do not need a $3,000 rifle, you need a $500 rifle and about $2,500 worth of training. If I hand the customer a rifle, I know is capable of tight groups at long ranges and they cannot shoot at least a 1-inch group at 50 yards then I usually recommend they take some rifle training and get back to the basics. Something as simple as their breathing could be all that they are doing wrong and a few classes later they can achieve the hits they want. The amount of time, work and expense that goes into accurizing a rifle amounts to wasted effort in the hands of a novice shooter. I do not recommend someone buy a precision rifle to learn basic rifle shooting because you are going to beat that rifle up during your training days and possibly destroy a great firearm. Most precision rifle barrels have a life span depending on how many rounds can be fired out of them and if you work through this training phase with this type of rifle then by the time you are a precision shooter, your rifle won't be. Learn with a decently priced rifle but still consider a durable, quality one. Once you can outperform that rifles capabilities then it may be time to invest in your "Long-Range Nail-Driver." If a customer wants me to create a precision rifle for them then I am going to. I am not usually in the business of turning customers away so I will take the sale, but I may want to talk to the customer more to determine their level of experience. If I can determine that their capabilities are not up to the standard needed to operate the precision rifle accurately then I will attempt to get even more business off the customer by offering classes to help them better understand how to use their new rifle.

Summarizing what occurs during the ejecting, cocking, feeding, and chambering operations.

So, let us begin with my description of ejecting. In most cases ejecting is the process in which the cartridge that was just fired is expelling the used casing from the firearm. With semi-automatic firearms there will usually be some type of ejector bar that kicks the used casing off the bolt face but in break action type firearms it is vastly different. If the break action has an ejector, it usually comes in the form of a piece of metal that springs the used casings out once the break action is fully open.

Next, we have my definition of cocking. This works very differently in a lot of different firearms but to define what is occurring I would say that after firing and upon the return of the bolt, the mechanism that fires the gun is reset to a ready to fire position. This is not to say that every firearm has a bolt. For example, a single action revolver once fired does not have the ability to re-cock the mechanism but can be manually re-cocked by the user pulling back on the hammer. If we were to look at a semi-automatic AR-15 we would see something quite different. The bolt carrier group recoiling backward pushes the hammer rearward enough to get it to catch on the rest of the fire control group thus resetting or cocking the firearm to a ready to fire position.

Feeding is an interesting one to discuss in my opinion. Not only is it a big part of the cycle of operation but it also needs to be one of the first things you do even before step one in the cycle. If the user has not fed the firearm with live cartridges first, then with the first trigger squeeze, there will be no cycle of operation. Feeding is the process in which the user or the firearm inserts live ammunition into the barrel of the firearm. In semi-automatic firearms this is usually done with some sort of box magazine. After the firearms bolt has recoiled rearward, the recoil spring sends the bolt forward again and it will strip the round from the magazine and feed it into the barrel. However, in pump action shotguns this feeding process works a little differently. Pump actions are tube fed usually and once the pump is pulled to the rear a lift bar is dropped, releasing one cartridge. When the pump is returned forward the leader or lift bar helps guide the round into the barrel.

Last, we have chambering to discuss. As the last step in the operation, it is important to note that if your firearm is out of ammunition, it will not chamber anything and will sometimes remain locked in an open position. Chambering is the process where the firearm takes its ammunition and locks it into the throat of the barrel in preparation to fire the next cartridge. Chambering in a semi-automatic AR-15 usually includes the bolt face, turning and locking the ammunition into the barrel were in a break action, the user must place a round back into the barrel and close the action. A lot of my definitions are kind of broad because not every firearm performs these actions the same.

Once specific safety and functions checks have been completed on a firearm, is it ready to be fired?

There may be many reasons for a test fire on a firearm. The first being the customer claims something is not working correctly with their firearm. In this case you may need to test fire to see the actual malfunction they were talking about in order to better understand the issue and find the best way to resolve it. In other cases, a test fire may be part of ensuring a firearm you built yourself actually functions. With an FFL that allows the manufacturing of firearms you can purchase all the parts you want for a build and assemble the firearm from scratch. This, however, means that you should test fire before selling the firearm to ensure the product being put out for sale is a functioning one.

As someone who has spent a number of years working for live fire facilities, I have seen countless firearms I was unfamiliar with and was then asked to clean, diagnose, or fire them. This can be a little unsettling at times especially when it is a much older firearm worth a fair bit of money. In such cases I would usually admit to the customer that I am new to this make or model and that it would take me some time to do the research to complete the task the correct way. Doing research is one of the best ways to make an unfamiliar firearm safe to test fire. The firearm may in great working order but if you the operator have no idea how it works it may yield unsafe results. Now if the customer is ok with someone who just admitted to knowing little about their firearm to complete the task, then do as you promised and take the time to do it right. At the very least, if you did make a mistake then you don't look like someone claiming to be a professional but having no clue.

Why malfunctions of blowback-operated firearms are often related to operator or ammunition issues.

Malfunctions with blowback type operation can occur for many reasons including both ammunition and operator error. If the ammunition did not have enough gunpowder in the casing when it was fired, you may end up with a failure to extract or failure to eject type malfunction. This could also result in a squib load where the bullet pushes from its casing but never exits the barrel. Without the energy required to blow back the slide or bolt on the firearm you may experience a short stroke that prevented the extraction and ejection of the casing. It is important that the person purchasing the ammunition knows the difference between factory ammunition and REMAN or remanufactured ammunition. Factory-made ammunition can still have this happen but not very often because of their quality checks in place to prevent this. If you decide to purchase remanufactured ammunition, you need to trust the manufacturer did so correctly. More often when I see issues with ammunition it is remanufactured.

Switching to the topic of operator error, if the user of the firearm has limp wrist when firing a pistol then the slide will short stroke and create a failure to eject type malfunction. This is also referred to as a stove pipe malfunction because when the spent casing gets caught in the ejection port it looks like a stove pipe coming out. The user must be able to manage the recoil of the pistol in order for proper operation to occur. If not holding the frame in place as the pistol recoils, then some of the energy required for a full cycle of the slide is gone and it will usually extract the spent casing but not eject it. Also, in some cases it may not re-cock the firearm or feed the next round of ammunition. As a gunsmith I would ask a series of questions to determine if the operator is the issue or if the ammunition is. Questions like how old the ammunition is and how it was stored will likely tell me if the ammunition is bad. Asking questions like is the casing getting stuck in the ejection port when firing may tell me it was operator error. Finally, test firing the firearm to see if you can recreate the malfunction the owner is complaining of may give you your answer as well. This makes it easier to identify what the actual problem is.

Author Nathan Fosters prescribed methods to remove the rifle as a variable.

I believe that if you follow Nathan Fosters Prescribed methods for testing, setup, and bedding a rifle correctly then it should remove the rifle as a variable. This is why I said earlier on that I would probably start with the shooter and see if they have the skill or ability to make the shot at the distance, they wish to achieve using an already proven accurate rifle. Too many times in my line of work I see individuals who purchase the top-of-the-line rifle and equipment only to find out that they have no idea how to get an accurate shot off with it. Nathan fosters not only gives the individual the correct way to do these things but will usually offer some kind of alternative way of achieving the same result. What I like about this is that the individual who may be attempting to do this themselves can pick the method that best suits their needs or comfort level and give it a shot. An example of this is when he suggests using an aluminum arrow shaft as a pillar when bedding a rifle (Foster, Page 128). This is something that a lot of people might have on hand already and will aid in someone's ability to better accurize the rifle thus taking the rifle as a variable out of the equation entirely.

What other variables might also contribute to issues with accuracy?

Taking the rifle out of the equation still leaves a number of different variables that can contribute to issues with accuracy. The shooter's ability, quality of the firearm or the ammunition being used, weather conditions, what caliber is being shot at what distance and the list goes on. Simply having an understanding of these factors may help someone to better understand why they may not be hitting their target come time to shoot at a distance.

Comparing and contrasting the lever-action firearm with the bolt-action and single-shot firearms.

When working with a lever action firearm you do have a number of issues that you would not see with single shot or bolt action firearms. Most bolt action firearms are magazine fed so making sure it is stripping and feeding correctly is important but as far as the action goes, the bolt and trigger assemblies can be rather simple to deal with. With most Single shot firearms, they are even easier to troubleshoot because it is usually a break action and does not include many moving parts. But when we get into troubleshooting lever action firearms there are a lot more moving parts. The lever action rifle has been around for a long time and the number of parts varies depending on the make, model, and year of production. In most cases the lever action is tube fed and that has its own set of issues especially if it has a side loading gate. On occasion the round is not pushed all the way in the feeding tube to catch but has made it past the loading gate and the ammunition gets stuck behind the gate preventing the user from loading another round until the malfunction is cleared. If loaded and cocked correctly, the elevator or lifter bar drops down to the feeding tube and the tube will eject one round for chambering. When the lever is closed it should lift the ammunition and the bolt face should push the aligned round into the chamber of the barrel. If this lifter bar does not drop or lift, then it will not cycle ammunition and will not fire. The number of moving parts is vastly different from most bolt or single shot firearms. Depending on the make, model, and year of the firearm you may run into a number of different issues, and these are just a few you would not see on those other platforms.

A detailed explanation of the soldering process used to install the ribs on a shotgun barrel.

When we start talking about adding ribs to a shotgun barrel, it is important to note that there are a number of ways to go about attaching them to your firearm. Two of the most common include a less permanent epoxy method and what can be the tedious soldering method. To summarize the epoxy method, all you would need to do is rough up the spots the ribs touch the barrel, mix your epoxy, and apply to the surfaces. Then just attach it to the barrel making sure it stays straight during the curing process and that an excess of glue does not squish out and harden. This can look bad and is hard to clean off sometimes.

The more permanent solution to attaching the ribs to a shotgun barrel is to use solder and flux to bond the two pieces of metal together. If this firearm had ribs previously then you will need to thoroughly clean the old spots where it used to be attached. If these are the first ribs to be attached, then find out exactly where they come in contact with the barrel and mark those spots. Smooth surfaces may not give anything for the solder to grip onto so rough up the marked spots being careful not to ruin the finish outside the marked spots. Once this is done use a degreaser to ensure the surfaces are completely clean. Once you are ready to attach the rib you can use soft iron wire to hold the rib in place, so it does not move during this next step. A wedge under the wire will hold tight to the rib and keep the rib flush with the barrel. Next, I can use a hand torch to heat the barrel slowly so I can apply some flux to the connection points. The flux allows the solder to bond the two pieces. When applying the solder, it is better to use more than you think you will need because using too little may give you sections of rib that are only partially attached. During the cooling process it is possible that some stress flexes the rib and if the rib is not fully soldered on then it can crack the bond and it may not remain connected or even straight. It is also important not to use it way too much because it will take some time to clean off the access solder off.

I have seen this process done once or twice in the past by a few people who do things a little differently. One-person would pre flux and solder the ribs connection points so when it is placed on the barrel, they are positive that there is solder all the way through the connection. Another person just kept alternating heat, flux, and solder in that order until they no longer saw the solder being pulled into the connection point by the flux. I believe both of these methods to be sufficient and allow for minimal cleanup after the barrel and ribs have cooled. Lightly tapping the connection point with a brass hammer and listening to the sound it makes can help you determine if there were any points in your connection that did not bond correctly.

Using a metal lathe to machine threads on a Remington 700 to attach a muzzle break.

So, a customer walks into the shop and has a Remington 700 with a stainless-steel barrel. They have a specific muzzle break they would like installed and have requested that we cut the threads for the muzzle break and install the part. To achieve this, you will need to Locate the threads, center the lathe, and make your cuts. Tools needed for this may include Calipers, rulers, squares, protractors, scribes, and layout dye. Also, I think it goes without saying that this is best done on a metal turning lathe.

One of the most important steps you can take during this whole process is when you plan the location of your threads. Check out the muzzle break and determine if you need a shoulder, shims, or a crush washer to attach it and consider this in your measurements. Please remember that you really only get one shot at doing this correctly so check your measurements and equipment multiple times throughout the process. Cover the muzzle in a thin coating of marking dye and allow it time to dry. This will be how you make your measurements directly on the muzzle end of the barrel. Use the scribe's rulers and protractors to begin marking the layout to include the length of the threaded area, thread relief and the shoulder. Again, be sure to double check every mark and measurement you make for accuracy.

If you decide to center the lathe, you will need a bar of heat-treated steel. First chuck the steel bar into the lathe jaws and be sure it is turned true. Once you have the bar mounted in the lathe you will set your compound rest to 60 degrees with the spindle moving in reverse. After that you will check the height of the cutting edge. This will need to be centered to ensure a true cut when milling.

And now we can begin the thread cutting work. You will want to move the cutter into a position where it is just barely touching the barrel. Be sure all measurements are correct one more time before you start cutting to avoid any mistakes. Once the cutter is touching the barrel you will need to reset your compound dial to zero. Move the carriage until the cutter is just past the barrels muzzle. Using the compound wheel, advance the cutter to the depth you want to cut. The next part should be done in multiple passes. turn the lathe on and use the apron wheel to move the cutter through the cuts stopping only at the shoulder you marked earlier. Set the compound to zero again, move the cutter back, check your measurements one more time and make your final pass. I have intentionally left out the measurements of the cuts you will need to make because this can change depending on the type of threads on the new muzzle brake, the size of the barrel you are working with and the caliber of the firearm.

Presenting the customer with options (rebarelling vs. lapping) when the customer has requested lapping.

A customer returned to your shop and informed you that his customized Remington M700's shot groups have considerably increased over his last few range sessions. While inspecting the bore, you noticed severe pitting from the chamber through to approximately 10" down the barrel. The customer informs me that he has recently started shooting corrosive surplus ammunition. After presenting the customer with his options (rebarelling vs. lapping) the customer has requested you lap his barrel.

The materials & tools required when lapping a barrel include calipers to take measurements, a hand torch, steel cleaning rod with a rotating handle, liquified lead and a means to pour it accurately, some oil and finally some lapping compound. Construction of the lapping rod may begin by wrapping a piece of cotton or twine around a section of steel cleaning rod and pushing this rod down the barrel until a few inches from the muzzle thus creating some kind of plug. Taking a low temp torch, heat up the barrel in a way that would melt solder but not damage the finish on the barrel. Now, using some melted lead and a ladle of sorts, pour a small amount into the barrel. This should imprint the rifles lands and grooves and melt the lead directly onto my steel cleaning rod.

So, with this new cleaning rod I have created, I will let it cool slightly but then I will push it about halfway out of the muzzle. Please be sure not to remove this entirely because you will need to start over again. If you find any burrs or damage to your rifling imprint, take a few files and be sure to take your time working them out. Now move the barrel in the vice to a position you can work the new lapping rod in and out of. Apply lapping compound to the rifled part of this lapping rod and add oil to the inside of the barrel. Begin to pull the lapping rod through until you reach the bore making sure not to completely remove the rod. Continue this back and forth adding more lapping compound as needed until the barrels rifling improves.

The process of turning a barrel blank using a conventional metal turning lathe.

To start, we will discuss what barrel contour is. You may have noticed that barrel's range in shape, size, weight, and profile. This can be for many reasons but one of the most common reasons you may see a contoured barrel is to cut the weight of a rifle down. A good example of this can be found on a variety of AR-15 rifles. Some states require that it come with a heavy barrel that keeps the same profile from bore to muzzle but these often weigh a lot more. Other states do not have such restrictions and will allow the AR-15 to be built with barrels that have much less material that weigh less and cool off much faster after use. The term barrel turning commonly refers to a gunsmith taking a blank of metal and chucking it into a lathe in order to machine off the excess metal and create the profile or contour they want.

To do this, you may want to use a bar of heat-treated steel for a lathe center. It is at this point that you may also want to face off or remove 1" from the muzzle end because the end may be flared from the boar reaming process. Now for this next step, the cutting tool used will vary from shop to shop but a slightly dull tool will cut far better than a sharp one in this case and the speed at which you run your lathe may depend on how the metal is supported. One method of barrel turning has you remove the center all together and chuck the barrel directly into the 3-jaw. The blank will then be turned in sections making your cuts close to the chuck and moving the blank multiple times.

Hogging off large amounts of material should be done in steps as well and not to be done all at once. Work one side then flip it in the chuck to hit the other side allowing time for the other half to cool while the opposite half is being worked. The type of tools used to work the barrel and the process you use to achieve this are going to change depending on the type of metal used. Finally, once you have a relative size and shape you can complete your final turning using a fine feed and a light cut. This is the final step so please take your time and be sure not to damage your final product.

Investigating the bedding of the barreled action to the stock for a Remington 700.

Usually, you would want a more permanent solution when bedding your barrel and action to the stock. However, Mock bedding can be done with epoxy and provides a semi-permanent solution if you wish to try this yourself. A rifle with no bedding at all may give the shooter wider shot groups at a distance and that is because the rifle's barrel is able to move as the shot is taken. This wobble may begin to occur before the bullet exits the muzzle. This can cause the muzzle to move in many different directions and prevent the shooter from creating a tight shot group. Mock bedding with epoxy would be considered a semi-permanent solution because it will fill those gaps between the rifles stock and the barrels locking lug. Find the spot on the stock where the barrels locking lug fits into and apply epoxy. Press in the barrel and action into the stock firmly to ensure bubbles are pushed out and a tight fit is achieved and allow time for the epoxy to cure. The reason this is considered semi-permanent solution is because once done it will hold very well but if the rifle is completely disassembled then once put back together the barrels locking lug will not be as secure as it was before, and you may need to repeat the epoxy bedding process again for a tight fit.

If at this point, I am sure that the crown and breach lock-up are repaired correctly and that the bedding is done to satisfaction then the next thing I may want to do is to inspect the rifling inside the barrel. Lead or nitro fouling may prevent the correct spin on the round before it exits the barrel and this can cause the bullet to wobble in flight making it less accurate especially at distance. It is also possible that the owner or even previous owners of this rifle did not take good care of it. Allowing rust to form inside the barrel and having that rust sit for a while allows the rust to start pitting into the metal and this may damage or destroy the rifling inside the barrel.

When bedding a rifle, should you free-float the entire barrel?

Explaining to the customer what you will be doing to their rifle during the bedding process.

If I were to explain to the customer what steps I would need to take to correctly bed their rifle, I would probably begin with the preparation it takes before applying the bedding compound. I would let them know that things like tape and putty would be used in order to prevent seepage that can be difficult to remove later on. I may need to explain what a pillar is and why I may need to use them during the bedding process. Talking to the individual and discussing the actual bedding process and the type of stock being used may determine what compound I will be using to get the best results, and this will also tell me if I need to add things like chopped up fiberglass for buildup or reinforcement in certain areas. Finally, I would discuss the cleanup stage and the areas of the firearm I may need to check for the correct finish and bedding.

Should you free-float the entire barrel? Why or why not? Remember that the lapped barrel is performing well on the mock-bedding.

The most common way most people do this today is to bed the action and free float the barrel. To get the best results you need pressure that remains constant and consistent as possible. This can be hard to achieve with a wood stock as it can be susceptible to things like moisture and humidity. If the barrel

I lapped is performing well on the mock bedding without any bedding done for the barrel, then it may be time to do a more permanent bed and consider free floating the barrel in general. Free floating the barrel ensures the barrel has no contact with the stock and this allows the barrel to whip naturally after a shot is taken. You just would not want to free float the barrel if the rifle is using a plastic stock with no bedding because the amount of movement that can occur after a shot will result in extremely poor accuracy.

The customer asks why you cannot just leave the rifle bedded as you did for the test-fire. Explain the difference between mock bedding and final bedding.

The reason for the mock bedding was to see if this temporary solution would fix the problem of poor accuracy. If done correctly and this yields better results, then it was clear that this was a major component in the rifle's inability to hit at distance and finishing the job with a more permanent bedding would be necessary. Mock bedding will loosen over time and will need to be done multiple times over the rifle's life span but if allowed to final bed the rifle with the correct solution then it should fire accurately for a long time with little to no upkeep.

Some gunsmiths will pin the grip safety in a collapsed or activated position, would you or should you do this?

As to whether I would consider pinning the grip safety on a 1911, though I do see this pinning method as a much more professional way to achieve this as opposed to the use of a rubber band, I would really need to contemplate whether I would or not. On the one hand, I would have individuals sign waivers that will not make me liable for anything done with the firearm or the type of work that was done, and the 1911 does still have a safety selector switch even if I override the grip safety, there is still a large part of me that screams not to do this. If the issue is that the customer has trouble activating it correctly then my first thought is usually, they need some training on the correct way to grip a firearm or a parts swap to solve the issue. Tough question though and I thank you for that.

Identifying two specialty tools that can be used in the 1911.

The two specialty tools used for the 1911 I have chosen for this week's discussion are the 1911 bench block and the lug fitting kit. While there are other bench blocks on the market advertised as universal, the one specifically designed for work on the 1911 has functions and features only meant for the 1911 platform. An example of this is the groove cut into the block specifically for use with the barrel and lug allowing easy removal and replacement of the pin that connects them.

Regarding the 1911 bench block and its use, you could probably manage the work without one but using one ensures ease of operation and you are less likely to damage any parts. This tool may require some special understanding to use it but nothing the user's manual cannot explain. For example, if you did not know that this cut was for the slide and that cut was for just the barrel, you may use it incorrectly and this may cause damage to the firearm and its parts. As far as engineering goes, I believe it depends on the brand you purchase. One may be well made and exhibit all the needed features while others may be cheap and miss important functions. Buy cheap and you will buy twice so look into a durable option with relevant features.

Talking about the lug fitting kit now, other traditional tools could be used to get the fitment correct but using the lug fitting tool kit makes the process easier and guarantees a more precise fit than the guess work that would happen using other tools. This tool is used to get a good fit between the barrels foot and its lug to the shaft of the slide stop. Having a general understanding of how this tool is used will help you from damaging the parts of your 1911 by overworking the components and creating a loose fit that may cause malfunction. Depending on the brand of lug fitting kit you purchase it may be cheap and only works a few times before it is so worn you are no longer getting a precise fit. Buy a durable well engineered fitting kit and it should last you a long time.

Three components within the 1911 platform and the answers to a few important questions.

The 3 components I have chosen include the trigger, firing pin and extractor.

The critical dimensions associated with these components & what potential malfunctions may occur if damage or improper modifications were made to the components.

The trigger has a bar connected to it that slides into a grove cut inside the frame and wraps around the magazine. If this is bent it may not fit into the groove cut in the frame or it may prevent a magazine from being inserted, making its dimensions critical to its operation. If the trigger being pressed does not contact the sear spring, then you get a failure to fire type malfunction.

The firing pin needs to be the appropriate length for the 1911 it is being used in and the correct width to fit in its channel with little room for movement that may prevent the tip of the pin from pushing through the breach face to strike the primer. Using a shorter pin designed for a compact 1911 in a full size will result in another failure to fire.

Is damage likely to these components and why?

- It can be hard to damage a 1911 trigger because of its simplicity but that is not to say it cannot break or be installed incorrectly.

- The extractor can break at the claw for many reasons to include firing steel cased ammunition or dropping a round in the barrel and slamming the slide forward.

- Firing pins can get worn down with prolonged use and abuse and on occasion can break in the firing pin channel of the slide.

Training a gunsmith should be done to avoid causing damage to these components.

I recommend taking the 1911 advanced armorers' course with Sonoran Desert Institute to get a better understanding of the 1911 platform and avoid causing damage to many of the 1911 parts. American Gunsmithing Institute is another great source for information on the 1911 platform.

The additional components, how they interact with the components I selected, and their critical dimensions.

The extractor is very simple and is held in place with a groove cut on the rear for the firing pin stop to slide into. This firing pin stop also helps retain the firing pin and firing pin spring allowing the rear of the firing pin to be exposed so the hammer can strike it and fire the cartridge in the barrel. Lastly, once the trigger is pressed the bar on the rear contacts the sear spring allowing the 1911 to release the hammer to strike the firing pin and fire the cartridge in the barrel.

Interesting aftermarket work that can be performed on a 1911 firearm.

Identifying interesting aftermarket work that can be performed on a 1911 firearm.

Turning the 1911 into what is sometimes called a race gun is one of the most detailed examples of after-market work you can do on this platform. It breaks down into categories such as optics and mounting, flared magazine wells for faster reloads, muzzle breaks and forward mounted weights to manage recoil. Some even add charging handles to the slide and checkered grips for faster operation and better control.

The one I chose as an example was from a google search of the words 1911 Race Gun. I am not in favor of this one over any other, but it had one of the best-looking examples that included a number of after-market parts installed. Most people who own one of these like competition style shooting and want a firearm they can manipulate fast and accurately. The addition of the flared magazine well can usually be done with the right part and an Allen key. Adding the charging handle to the slide can be done with a CNC cut and the right part but I have even seen ones that replace the rear iron sight. Depending on the manufacture of the side mounted optics plate, mounting procedures vary but always screw to the frame, so the optic does not recoil with the slide after the shot. The muzzle break that is available to the 1911 platform may push gas up or out but not usually down. The purpose of this is to disperse the gas in a direction that keeps the muzzle flip relatively flat during operation for faster follow-on shots. Some people like Checkering the frames grips and changing the grip panels to make for a more aggressive texture while others add metal rail thumb rest so they can loosen up their grip and still maintain a safe and accurate grip.

Outlining cons that may be associated with this work if it is not performed properly.

One of the biggest cons is that the more changes you make to the original design, the more likely you are to have issues and trying to break down exactly what could be going wrong with its operation could end up being the fault of the after-market stuff you added. Additionally, these are usually so fine-tuned that something like changing the ammunition type could cause malfunction as well.

How the firearms industry benefited from the 1911 platform.

Browning held the patent for the grip safety used in the 1911 handgun along with a number of other parts. Fast forward to today and we see companies like Smith & Wesson shield models that use the same type of technology not to mention that it is still a standard part in most current production 1911's.

This firearm has advanced the firearms industry tremendously since its creation. The 1911 showed the world that you can make an affordable firearm with very few parts and still be able to trust your life to its operation. Throughout the years this platform has been tweaked and modified in countless ways by many different manufactures showing the industry that if you start with good bones then the sky is the limit regarding modifications. Today you find manufacturers making the latest and greatest 2011 models that originated from the older 1911 platform. Staccato Offers top of the line 2011 models in any variation you want, and these models would not exist today if it were not for John Browning's 1911.

Identifying three component interactions within the 1911 that I found interesting & why I found these interactions so intriguing.

To start, I think the trigger bar that wraps the magazine well is interesting. The way it slides into a groove from the rear of the frame has got to be one of the easiest triggers I have ever had to install on a handgun. The simplicity of its operation in the 1911 also makes it very reliable. Next, I thought it was interesting that both grip safety and safety selector switch are connected through the frame via the pin on the selector switch itself. The way these two safety components work in tandem helps ensure the firearm the safe operation for its user. Finally, I thought the extractor was interesting because of its simplicity as well. No additional springs and the fact that it is one piece make it reliable and easy to replace if it becomes worn or damaged from prolonged use.

A customer has requested you service his favorite family heirloom—a World War II Arisaka Type 2.

Your customer has requested you service his favorite family heirloom—a World War II Arisaka Type 2 Paratrooper rifle (also called a TERA—Teishin Rakkasan Assault/Raiding Paratrooper). After you take note of the serial number, you notice the retaining pin used to secure the barrel/forearm assembly to the receiver appears to be missing the D-ring. The D-ring is intended to aid the shooter in pulling the wedge to disassemble the rifle for transportation. After bringing it to the customer's attention, he has requested you create the D-ring.

If you cannot find a physical sample or blueprint of a part you are trying to create, this may help you get a measurement for the part.

If I were not able to find any schematics or blueprints for a specific part I was trying to create, I would need to find another way to find the measurements for the part. You can start by looking at some older catalogs for the firearm in question. With the invention of the internet came endless knowledge and resources. Most things have been scanned and uploaded nowadays and with the right amount of searching you can find them. Even if the owner's manual has not been printed for 100 years, there will be someone out there who had the training material and has uploaded it. However, some firearms companies choose not to release their firearms schematics, and this makes things a little harder. If this is the case, you may need to find a friend or another customer with the same firearm and ask them to inspect it for the part you were missing. This would allow you to get the exact dimensions of the part and even tell you what the part was made of. All else fails, start measuring the space the part occupied and make the new part based on those measurements. This can take some trial and error so take your time.

Determining the material to construct the part from is easy in some cases.

It can assume that the part needed to fix the missing component on this World War II Arisaka Type 2 Paratrooper rifle would be made of steel. This is not always going to be the case, but this missing d ring on the pin that connects the barrel and foregrip to the rifle's action and stock needs to be durable. This is the pin that threads into the rifle during assembly and not having the d ring to tighten or loosen the threaded pin can be a pain. A softer metal like lead or aluminum being used for this purpose could bend, break, or become distorted because the connection point is prone to stress while carrying and general usage. It is possible the original was a different metal, and this is the reason it is missing. By knowing the purpose of the part, you can usually determine what material should be used to create it.

How would you test the part for quality?

Beginning with a high-quality steel usually is a good place to start if attempting to create a good quality part. Once the part has been machined you can check its fit and finish to ensure that the piece you created meets the need of the part that was broken or missing. Knowing it is a quality metal and that it fits my needs I would then move on to test firing the rifle but only if the customer intends to use the firearm. Because this is a family heirloom, it may not ever need to fire so be clear with your customer as to whether they want a functioning rifle or just a display one.

Answering several questions that demonstrate knowledge of key principles related to troubleshooting.

The first thing you must know before attempting to disassemble or inspect a firearm.

The first thing I would want to know before attempting to disassemble or inspect a firearm is how to clear it of ammunition. Some firearms like Glocks require the user pull the trigger to remove the slide and being sure the firearm is not loaded is the first and most critical step.

In a straight blowback system, when does the bolt/slide begin reacting to the pressure created by the ignited cartridge and what does this teach us about the importance of timing?

When the primer is struck there is not enough pressure to cycle the slide or bolt for normal operation. Burning gunpowder and building pressures push both forward and backward, pushing the bullet out of the muzzle and pushing the casing out of the bore starting its extraction and ejection process. The exact moment the bolt or slide reacts to this pressure is when the bullet exits the muzzle. Timing is important because if the pressure is too much as the casing is being extracted then the casing wall may expand or crack causing malfunctions.

Explain how the rollers in the roller-delayed blowback system delay the opening of the action.

The rollers in a roller delayed blow-back system works like a locking lug. In the forward position the rollers push into grooves and help to ensure the firearm is in battery before being fired. This delays blowback because it requires a little more pressure to push the rollers in and then allow the slide or bolt to cycle.

Identify one modern firearm that uses the gas-delayed blowback system and explain how the gas is used to delay the system.

The Walther CCP 9mm uses the Gas-Delayed blowback system. This system uses a small hole just after the bore of the barrel to allow some gas to escape while pushing the projectile out of the muzzle. The pressure will eventually transfer to the slide for normal operation but this little bit of gas that escapes can delay the blowback of the slide. Walther calls this Softcoil instead of recoil.

Levers are typically used to create a mechanical advantage. How do the levers in the lever-delayed blowback system do just the opposite?

The lever used in the lever-delayed blowback operating firearms creates a mechanical disadvantage. This lever is internal and rotates until it unlocks the bolt or slide allowing freedom of motion for extraction and ejection of the spent casing. The time it takes to unlock or rotate that lever creates the delay.

At what point in a blowback system is the firearm considered "locked"?

The term used here is just blowback system and the term locked could mean a few things depending on the firearm. In general, the firearm is considered locked when the slide or bolt are closed all the way or in battery. If the firearm uses any of the other delayed blowback systems it would be considered locked when the rollers, levers or lugs are in their closed locked positions.

Is it always true that blowback systems are reserved for low-pressured cartridges? If not, what is an example of a firearm that is chambered for a high-pressure cartridge and uses the blowback system?

At first thought my brain screamed Barret 50Cal. The Model 82A1 is an example of a firearm that is chambered in one of the largest calibers I have shot, and this model uses a reciprocating bolt and is a semi-automatic type of rifle. Barret does make the Model 95 that is a bolt action rifle, but I do not recommend it.

Summarizing the detail-stripping process of a Glock pistol.

My goal of a detailed stripping of a firearm is to get it broken down to as many pieces as possible. This ensures that no part goes untouched and allows me to inspect each part for damage or filth. Once everything is taken apart, I will usually clean everything just to be sure that when it is reassembled it is in good working order.

List the reference materials you used to complete the procedure.

As I have a ton of experience with Glock firearms in my day-to-day work and the fact that I am a certified armorer, I did not need any reference materials. If I were to recommend some to people with less experience, I would say take a look at Glocks website for downloadable material. This covers a lot of different topics and will get you acquainted with the firearm and its parts. Then look at the Glock Reference Guide, 1st & 2ND Edition written by Robb Manning because this covers everything the owner's manuals will not.

How far were you able to make it through detail-stripping before requiring a specialty tool that you did not have access to?

Luckily, I had all the tools required to complete the detailed stripping of the Glock 17 Handgun. This is not always going to be the case though because some firearms have extremely specific tools made just for that make and model. If I remember correctly the IWI Tavor requires a weapon specific wrench to complete the disassembly process.

What additional tools did you need to completely detail-strip your firearm?

The tools required to detail strip a Glock pistol are simple. A punch, Hammer and maybe a small flathead for leverage on a few parts and that is it. This differs from a field strip in the fact that field stripping a Glock handgun requires no tools at all.

Did you find any steps in the progress particularly difficult? Were there any specific cautions you had to be mindful of to avoid damaging the firearm? How did you overcome those challenges?

The most difficult part for me on the Glock Gen 4 is during the reassembly process. When putting one of the pins back through the frame it must feed through the hole on the slide catch and the tiny spring bar needs to be pushed down while inserting the pin so as to be under the pin for the proper spring tension to exist.

Compare your results with the plan you created. Did your plan help you with this project? Did the process and results match your expectations?

After comparing my results with the plan, I made initially I am happy to say everything worked out just fine. There were no broken or missing parts, and everything was disassembled and reassembled as expected. It is important to note that anytime you plan on working on any firearm, you have a plan. Grouping your parts, labeling things, or recording yourself in the process are just a few ideas you should consider in your planning process. This usually helps to prevent losing parts and helps you figure out what pins and screws go to what parts.

Ruger 10/22 "doesn't seem to want to kick out the brass."

A customer brings you the following rimfire carbine. He says it has worked reliably for years, but recently it "doesn't seem to want to kick out the brass." He says it ejects some of the time, but not always, and the problem is getting worse. When questioned, he says he is not sure if there is a particular type of ammo this happens with, but he doesn't think so.

Making the firearm safe to begin working on it.

While keeping the firearm pointed in a safe direction, I would use the magazine release button to remove the feeding source. Next, I would use the charging handle located on the side of the bolt and I would pull it to the rear and using the toggle by the trigger guard, I would lock the bolt to the rear. Finally, I would both visually and physically inspect the chamber for the presence of ammunition.

If, during the test fire, you discover that the problem the customer complained of persists with multiple types of ammunition, what other parts do you need to inspect?

Assuming we are talking about already having replaced the ejector bar, the next likely part I would inspect is the extractor. It is possible that it has worn down and only partially grabs the rim of the round. This slippage of the rim during extracting may cause an issue with the ejecting of the casing as well.

Describing the type of failure, what components caused the malfunction, the components you could remove/replace, and the tests that may be performed to verify operation:

The type of malfunction you were experiencing was actually a failure to extract which also led to the failure to eject you spoke of. This failure to "kick out the brass" was due to a dirty gun and a worn extractor. The carbon buildup that happens with these Ruger 10/22 rifles is a lot considering how small the ammunition is, so the bore of your barrel was dirty enough to get casings stuck. Couple this with an extractor that has worn down over the years of use and we found your issue. After a detailed cleaning and having installed a replacement extractor the firearm works as intended again. Keep your firearm clean and it should run reliably for the next few years.

A customer brings you a Benelli Vinci and explains that it will not feed shells.

Making this firearm safe to begin working on it.

Starting with the safety selector being pushed into a safe position and keeping the firearm pointed in a safe direction I would inspect the feeding tube for the presence of ammunition. Then I would use the bolts charging handle and locking it to the rear I would physically and visually inspect the chamber for ammunition. Once I was sure it was free of ammunition I would continue with my work.

The procedures & processes you should follow to eliminate user error or ammunition as the cause of the malfunction.

Making sure the firearm is held tightly in the pocket of the shoulder of the shooter ensures the inertia of the fired shell is transferred to the bolt and not lost in a loose grip. I could test fire myself or watch the owner shoot to determine if this was the issue. Next, I would try a few different shot types and weights to see if the firearm just dislikes a particular round.

Note: Inertia-driven shotguns have multiple intricate parts that can cause a failure to feed if they are damaged or bent, and it would be impractical for you to list them all here. For this assignment, list one possible part that might cause this malfunction.

The carrier or elevator bar that is supposed to take the next round from the feeding tube to the barrel could be to blame. If the shell being fired works and the shooter is doing everything correct but it is not cycling the next round it is possible that the lifter is not pushing up on the shell to chamber the next shot.

The test you could perform after making such a repair and what you should hope to learn by doing this.

I would start with snap caps to ensure the carrier was lifting the shell as intended. Once I was sure this works, I would take the rounds I know to work well with this firearm, and I would test fire on a live fire facility and see if it cycles correctly thus fixing the customers stated issue.

A customer brings you a Browning Hi Power and explains that it does not fire.

The customer brings you a Browning Hi Power and explains that it does not fire when the hammer falls on a loaded chamber. He states that the hammer does reach full cock when cycling the slide and manually cocking the hammer itself.

Making this firearm safe to begin working on it.

Like most 1911 type firearms this browning high power has a safety selector switch that locks into a groove on the slide. Keeping the firearm pointed in a safe direction push the magazine release and remove the feeding source. Next push the selector to fire to unlock the slide and with your finger off the trigger, pull the slide to the rear. Use the slide catch to lock it to the rear and visually and physically inspect for the presence of ammunition.

The procedures & processes you should follow to eliminate user error or ammunition as the cause of the malfunction.

This is when a test fire would be needed. I am positive in my ability to work the firearm without user error being an issue. Couple this with me testing the ammunition they provided, and I should be able to recreate the malfunction or prove that the customer was doing something wrong while firing. On occasion I will have the owner fire the pistol with me watching so I can see what they may be doing right or wrong that could cause the issue they are describing.

The part I would most suspect to be causing this failure and why.

If I had determined that the ammunition they are using is still good and it had to be partly to blame for the pistol not firing I would look at the firing pin first. If the pistol has a working trigger and hammer, then it is possible the firing pin is broken or worn, and the energy of the falling hammer is not being transferred to the primer of the cartridge.

Tests you could perform after making the replacement and what you may hope to learn.

A funny test I see people do to ensure they are getting a strike with the firing pin is popping a pencil down the barrel of a firearm that has already been cleared and pulling the trigger. If it is striking the eraser, it should throw the pencil out of the barrel. Then of course I would step onto the range and do a live fire test to ensure everything is firing as intended.

Savage Model 110 chambered in 7mm Remington Magnum Troubleshooting.

The customer brings you a Savage Model 110 chambered in 7mm Remington Magnum. The rifle appears to have been poorly maintained. Customer states that the rifle has been "misfiring a lot, lately."

Upon further conversation, you get the additional information from her:

- By "misfire," she means that the rifle does feed ammunition, but does not discharge a round when the trigger is pulled. She states the problem has been intermittent but getting worse.

- She has tried multiple brands and models of ammunition but has not noticed a difference from one to another.

How to safely remove/clear the magazine, chamber, and barrel of ammunition and obstructions.

Starting by making sure the firearm is safe, I would then remove the feeding source to ensure I am not loading more ammunition in the process. I would then rotate the bolt and pull it rearward to expose the chamber of the barrel and make sure there was no live ammunition present. Finally, I would use a bore light to be sure the firearm is free of obstructions.

Initial Inspection and Diagnosis

The action type of the firearm in question is a bolt action. The most likely failure on the firearm is simply a dirty firearm. If the problem is intermittent and continues to get worse and worse than it is likely the components of the firearm are moving sluggish due to carbon buildup and the more it is fired the more it continues to build up carbon on key components.

A cool trick I learned years ago was to put sticky paper on the back side of a snap cap so you can see the punch of the primer without having to head to the live fire portion of the testing yet. If I get different results on the multiple firing pin strikes, then I can begin to focus there.

If a component were damaged, what component would be most suspected and why?

I believe that if a component was damaged in this case scenario, then it may be the firing pin. It is possible that the firing pin is there but broken in the firing pin channel. This means the hammer striking the rear of the pin may push the parts to the appropriate distance to strike the primer on the round but in some cases it would not. It is also possible that the pin is not broken but rounded off or compressed and again is giving the user intermittent firing.

If the part you identified needed replacement, where might you find a replacement and how much would this component cost?

Assuming it is the firing pin that was damaged and not just a dirty firearm, Brownell's and other companies do not carry the firing pin for the Model 110 chambered in 7mm as far as I could find. This would be one of those times I would reach out to the manufacturer and find the correct part needed. They may have more insight on the issue and be able to help but they should definitely have the correct part.

H&R Ultra chambered in .223 Troubleshooting.

How to safely remove/clear the magazine, chamber, and barrel of ammunition and obstructions.

Starting by making sure the rifle is safe, I would then push the locking lever and breach the barrel from the action face. Because this is a single shot brake action rifle, I would inspect to be sure a round is not still in the barrel and I may use a bore light to be sure the barrel has no obstructions in it. Once I am sure it is clear of ammunition, I will continue my work.

Serious damage that you might inspect for prior to moving forward with the troubleshooting process.

In clearing the firearm, you need to push the locking lever to breach the barrel. If this is not in good working order, you will not be able to open the firearm to ensure it is clear of ammunition.

Initial Inspection and Diagnosis

The action type of the firearm in question is a Break Action, Single Shot rifle. The most likely type of failure the customer is describing is simple. Because the customer said it is not ejecting the spent casing I would look at the lift bar and its parts to ensure it is not dirty or broken. I would not begin to look at things like the firing pin because the customer said it fires but just that the issue was ejecting.

I would more likely use snap caps chambered in the rifles caliber to recreate the customers' complaint. This is the safest way to do this because it uses the same type of ammunition but is inert and will not fire if a mistake was made. If it will not eject the snap cap, then I will be able to see what has gone wrong with the rifle.

The various tests you could perform may yield different results in this situation because the snap cap will not fire like live ammunition, I may not see the casing expand in a worn out bore and I would not see the problem in testing. If everything works fine using snap caps, I will then move on to a live fire test to see if the issue is reproduced. Once fired I can inspect the casing for damage that may show me the issue.

What may be the leading issue causing this platform to experience the type of failure we identified & why I think this.

In my experience it is usually a dirty firearm that creates the issue. The customer stated that he had fired this for years which means he has had it for a long time. This may not necessarily mean a worn-out barrel because it is a single shot firearm and I suspect it has not been shot to excess. My guess is that they have no idea how to disassemble those parts and the lifter bar that extracts the fired casing is stuck from carbon build up.

If a component were damaged, what component would be most suspected and why?

The lifter bar itself may have been rounded off after years for use and it may be slipping the rim of the casing and not ejecting it. This would probably be the first thing I would check after clearing the firearm.

Assuming the auto eject assembly was the cause of the malfunction, in a short customer summary, I will describe the type of failure, what

components caused the malfunction, the components I removed/replaced, and the tests that were performed to verify operation:

After taking the time to clear the firearm of ammunition and obstructions I was able to start looking at the components of the firearm that specifically deal with the ejecting of spent casings. Upon doing so I noticed your auto eject assembly was stuck and not moving to eject the casing. After disassembling it and cleaning the components it began to move as it is supposed to. In the final phase of working on the firearm I looked for broken or worn parts. It is possible your lift bar has been rounded down from years of use and I recommend replacing it with a more reliable ejection.

The M203 (make, model, action type) and the resources I used to find information on it.

The Lewis Machine & Tool M203 Grenade Launcher. Though it falls into the category of a destructive device and required me to get a tax stamp from the ATF to own, the AFT list this as an "NFA Firearm" so I believe it meets the criteria of a firearm. As I have already listed the make and model of "firearm" I will add that it has been in service since 1969 and is a single-shot, breech-loaded, pump action (sliding barrel), shoulder-fired weapon that fires multiple types of 40MM rounds.

Before anyone asks, no I do not have any live grenades for this "firearm" and would not even know where to fire something like that here in the states. I will be reaching out to LMT directly for the owner's manual on this one but in doing some research I was able to find the Army's Field Manual that has a ton of information on this weapon system and its uses. One of the biggest challenges I ran into was finding an exploded view of this particular weapon system, but I am sure this is because the Army and ATF REALLY do not want the general public to know the ins and outs of a grenade launcher.

While it is a lot easier to find and purchase a 37MM Launcher, I was working for an FFL who happened to pick this up and I could not pass on the opportunity to own the actual M203 40MM Grenade Launcher. Let me know if you think this was a bad choice.

Browning Buck Mark Troubleshooting.

Customer brings me a Browning Buck Mark that is experiencing a failure to extract. He says he has only tried one type of ammunition since purchasing the pistol.

Making this firearm safe to begin working on it.

First, I would remove the magazine so I would not feed ammunition to the firearm. Next, I would pull back on the slide and use the slide stop to lock it to the rear. Finally, I would visually and physically inspect the pistol for the presence of ammunition paying close attention to the exposed bore of the barrel.

"Short stroking," how it is caused, and the steps within the Cycle of Operations that can negatively affect this firearm.

Short stroking is when the bolt or slide of the firearm does not fully cycle. This usually results in the stove pipe or failure to eject type malfunction. You can tell when a firearm is short stroking because it may catch the spent casing in the ejection port, fail to feed the next round or even fail to re-cock the firearm.

During the test fire, you discover that the pistol experiences erratic extraction with a variety of ammunition & the part I would most suspect to cause this malfunction.

Erratic extraction when using different brands of ammunition may mean that something is wrong with the firearm and not the ammunition. One of the first things I would inspect for damage or missing parts would be the extractor located on the right side of the frame on the front of the slide. If it shows wear or is broken this may be why you have unpredictable or erratic extraction.

Based on the component that I identified as suspect; this is how I might remedy this malfunction.

Usually before I start looking to order parts I will clean the firearm to see if it was just dirty and not functioning as intended. Then I would test fire it again to see if the problem was fixed. If I did need to replace the part, then I would absolutely do some research on how it is done properly. I do not believe Mastery is required to perform this task, but it cannot hurt to research first.

The test you might want to perform after making such a repair and what you hope to learn by doing this.

Because we worked on the extractor, we can test to see if it works using snap caps. If it works that way, then it is time to hit the range and see what happens during normal operation with live ammunition. By test firing I can ensure proper operation of the extraction process and if the problem persists, I know the extractor is not the issue and I look for other reasons it was malfunctioning.

Ruger New Model Blackhawk Troubleshooting.

The customer brings you a Ruger® New Model Blackhawk® and claims that it does not fire when he pulls the trigger. He says that the hammer seems to be working; it locks back, and it falls when he pulls the trigger.

How to safely clear the chambers and barrel of ammunition and potential obstructions.

There are two ways to inspect this single action revolver for the presence of ammunition. The first being opening the loading gate and turning the cylinder until you have inspected every chamber in the cylinder. The second being to pull the center bar out that links the cylinder to the frame. This is located just under the barrel and requires you press a spring-loaded lock bar to remove the pivot bar. Then open the loading gate and the entire cylinder will come out. As far as clearing the barrel for obstructions goes, you can use a bore light at one end of the barrel to look for light coming out the other side. You could also insert a cleaning rod to see if there are any stoppages if a bore light is not available.

The Ruger Blackhawk is a single action only type revolver. The Ruger New Model Black Hawk does have a transfer bar as part of its operation. A "light strike" is a potential cause of this malfunction. A light strike is a failure to fire type malfunction. Though it may not be the ammunition that is the problem. More likely the firing pin is worn down or cracked or the transfer bar is not lifting to the correct position to allow the connection of the hammer and firing pin.

How to detect a "light strike" type malfunction.

After pulling the trigger and watching the hammer fall with no round being shot the user should hold the firearm in a safe direction for an additional few second just in case a hang fire occurs. Once you are sure the ammunition is not going to fire, empty the cylinder and inspect the primer on the casing. If the dent left is less than those casing that did fire this may mean that the firing pin did not hit the priming cup into its anvil and the priming compound did not ignite.

The components that you might suspect if the transfer bar is not functioning properly.

On occasion the transfer bar is bent and gets hung up on the bottom of the firing pin. The trigger will pull about halfway, and you would notice a stoppage in the pull due to the transfer bar hitting the bottom of the firing pin instead of sliding in front of the firing pin as intended.

Another component that you might suspect may cause a failure to fire in this type of revolver may be the cylinder lock. The transfer bar is definitely one of the main components that can cause this firearm to not fire but it could also be a number of different things like the cylinder lock slipping the notch and the round is misaligned and the firing pin struck the casing and not the primer.

Colt Python Troubleshooting.

The customer brings me a Colt® Python® and explains that the hammer will not reach full cock and falls prematurely.

How to safely clear the chambers and barrel of ammunition and potential obstructions.

This firearm is a double action revolver that has a cylinder release located on the side of the frame. This one you would pull rather than push and then the cylinder will swing free of the frame using a swivel arm. Then I would both visually and physically clear the chambers of the cylinder and take a bore light to ensure there are no obstructions in the barrel.

The Colt Python is a double action type revolver and based on the observation that the hammer does not reach full cock; the sear or sear catch is the likely cause of the failure. Because the hammer is falling prematurely it is my belief that the issue is with the sear surfaces.

Describing the type of failure, what components caused the malfunction, the components I might remove/replace, and the tests that can be performed to verify operation:

While inspecting the firearm I came across what I believe to be the issue with regard to the hammer not locking to the full cocked position. It is my belief that the failure to cock type malfunction is because the sear surfaces on the hammer has rounded off making it difficult to stay locked in the full cocked position. This would also explain why your hammer tends to fall prematurely because it is slipping off the required notch. Fixing the sear surface or replacing the hammer would solve the issue and allow the firearm to work as intended.

Winchester Model 1897 Troubleshooting.

A customer has brought you the following Winchester Model 1897. It is clean and well oiled, but very worn. The customer explains that when she works the action, the hammer does not stay back – it simply moves forward with the action. You confirm this by attempting to work the action yourself.

How to safely clear the feed source, chamber, and barrel of ammunition and potential obstructions.

First, I would make sure the firearms safety was on and working. Then I would attempt to clear the feeding tube located below the barrel by keeping the firearm pointer in a safe direction and flipping it upside down. You should be able to see if ammunition is loaded in the tube because you will either see an empty tubes follower or the head of the cartridge. If rounds are present in the feeding tube press the bar that catches and retains the cartridge located under the shotgun's bolt. This will allow ammunition to eject the feeding tube one at a time and is a safer way to unload it compared to cycling the rounds through the pumping action. Once I am sure there is no ammunition in the feeding source, I would then pull the pump to the rear exposing the chamber of the barrel and I would both visually and physically check for the presence of a round.

Initial Inspection and Diagnosis

The Winchester Model 1897 is a Pump Action shotgun. After reviewing the customer's complaint, based on my knowledge and research of firearms, The hammer should stay in the cocked position when the action is cycled. This type of failure is mechanical in nature and would have nothing to do with the ammunition.

This type of malfunction is most likely a failure to cock. When the pump is operated correctly the hammer will stay cocked until the trigger is pulled. With the hammer moving forward with the action the connector that is supposed to catch the hammer is not working. However, and this is a big one, it is possible the malfunction is operator error. This firearm has what is referred to as a slam fire. If the customer is holding the trigger as the pumping action is occurring, then the slamming of the pump closed would fire the next round Or allow the hammer to move with the action.

Detailed Assessment

If I were to determine that a part is the issue and this was not operator error, I may say that the hammer or hammer catch is the problem. If the hammer has excessive were like the rest of the firearm it is possible that the flat section that is supposed to catch and cock the hammer is rounded off and this will prevent it from locking correctly. It is also possible that the part that is supposed to lock with the hammer to cock it is broken, bent, rounded, or missing and this too would prevent it from cocking correctly.

I am afraid Snap Caps will not help with this one. For this job I would need to break down the firearm and do a detailed inspection of its parts. I have handled these firearms in the past and have a pretty good understanding of what the parts look like in good working order.

Assuming worn hammer notches were the cause of the malfunction, I will describe the type of failure, what components caused the malfunction, the components you removed or replaced, and the tests that were performed to verify operation:

The malfunction you were experiencing was a failure to cock the firing mechanism. This can be common in this type of firearm because they are often abused when slam firing the weapon system. During my detailed inspection I noticed excessive were to the hammer notches that are there to cock the hammer during normal operation. After repairing or replacing this hammer I was able to determine that the issue first discussed has been resolved and now when the pump action is worked, the hammer remains cocked until the trigger is pulled.

Early-1900's Winchester 1892 Troubleshooting.

A customer brings you an early-1900's Winchester 1892 that he recently inherited. He states that it has been in his father's gun cabinet for at least 50 years, and he cannot remember the last time he saw his father take it out. Besides a little surface rust, the rifle appears to be in fairly good working order. The customer's complaint is that the rifle is not feeding when he charges the action. He claims he can "get it to work once in a while, but not consistently." He has only attempted one type of ammunition, that he found in the drawer of his father's gun cabinet. He has not fired the rifle since inheriting it; he is only tried to cycle ammunition.

How to safely clear the feed source, chamber, and barrel of ammunition and potential obstructions.

First, I would make sure the firearms safety was on and working. With leaver actions that function using a feeding tube you often have a knob on the end of the tube the user can turn and pull the tube and spring out. Then the ammunition can slide out of the tube at the muzzle end of the rifle. Some models allow you to remove the ammunition through that loading gate used to load the firearm. By pressing all the way down on the gate, the ammunition loaded in the tube will eject one at a time. Once I am sure there is no ammunition in the feeding source, I would then open the cocking leaver exposing the chamber of the barrel and I would both visually and physically check for the presence of a round.

Initial Inspection and Diagnosis

The 1900's Winchester 1892 is a Lever Action. The most likely type of failure the customer is describing is a failure to feed. This sounds like the most likely reason the user cannot get the rifle to load correctly when he "charges the action." We cannot determine if it has failed to fire yet because the client has said they have not fired it since inheriting it.

"Short stroking" a lever action, how it is caused, and the steps within the Cycle of Operations that can negatively affect this firearm.

Short Stroking is something that falls into the category of operator error. This is when someone using a lever action is not cocking the leaver all the way open but rather is only using maybe half the needed "stroke" on the leaver for proper operation. This can affect the feeding and ejecting portions of the cycle of operation. If the lever action is not fully cocked the round may never be dropped onto the lifter bar to chamber a round. Also, when a round is fired, and the lever is not used correctly then the spent casing may be extracted but without the full cock of the lever the bolt may not reach a point to eject the casing from the firearm.

Short stroking could absolutely be the customer's issue. Remember the client has only tried cycling ammunition but still has not tried to fire it yet. If it is loading sometimes and not others it is very possible, they are not opening the action all the way with every stroke, and it is loading ammunition intermittently.

After verifying that the firearm is safe and prior to disassembling it, there are tests that you should perform.

Yes, there are a few tests we can try before heading to the range or breaking down a firearm. The customer has stated that the rifle feeds sometimes but not others so I would determine the caliber of the firearm and grab inert training ammunition like Snap Caps and try to recreate the issue with the client just to confirm what the issue was with them. This allows me the opportunity to test the rifle's ability to feed, chamber, lock, unlock, extraction and ejection in a safe way. It is possible I ran into an issue the customer has not yet and that created the issue the customer was complaining about in the first place.

Detailed Assessment

If I were expecting something to be wrong with any part of the firearm it would be the feeding spring in the feeding tube. These are often very long and do not put a ton of pressure on the rounds in the first place. Someone like the client's father may have left the rifle loaded for a long time and the prolonged compression on that spring may have caused damage. No push from the feeding spring and no next round especially if the muzzle is pointed down and rounds need to push straight up.

Post-inspection and repairs

Often, I will stop work at the point where I have fixed the issue that was discussed with the client. If during my repair work, I see other things that need to be addressed I will later inform the customer that these things may create future issues. But if the customer's issue was with the feeding of the firearm and that alone, then once I have finished my repair, I would not feel the need to test fire the rifle. The customer asked me to address every part of the cycle of operation except the firing portion so I would leave that to them especially with regard to something that could be considered a family heirloom. They may not want it fired and have not asked me to do so.

Assuming a worn lever was the cause of the malfunction, I will describe the type of failure, what components caused the malfunction, the components I might remove/replace, and the tests that will need to be performed to verify operation:

The type of failure you were experiencing was due to a worn leaver that was not allowing the internal components of the rifle to cycle correctly. After a detailed inspection of all of the parts in the rifle I spotted excessive wear on the lever itself that was not dropping your elevator or "lifter" bar correctly and this is why it would load sometimes and not others. The extractor hook and ejector look to be in good working order as we did not experience any issues with these operations. Also, the loading tube, spring and follower seem to be in good working order as well, so I installed a new lever and tested the rifle for consistent operation. It is my belief that the issue we discussed is now fixed and if they need any more help with the rifle, to swing back in and I would be glad to help.

Unbeknownst to the customer in Part 1, the Winchester had a badly worn firing pin and would not have fired if he had tried. I will be using my answers from Part 1 to respond to the following.

Diagnosing an unreported malfunction:

At what point in the previous section did you perform a test-fire and why did you do so if it was not brought to you for a failure to fire? If you did not perform a test-fire in the previous section, do you believe that you should have?

At no point in my previous assessment did I perform a test fire of the customer's rifle. Because the initial complaint was about feeding issues and not firing issues it was not necessary to fix the issue that was addressed. I stand firm in my not testing the firearms ability to fire initially however, if firing was addressed the first time, I would have done things with more focus on the firing pin and the rifles hammer and hammer spring as well.

I would not have discovered the issue with the worn firing pin when focusing on the feeding, chambering, locking, unlocking, extracting, or ejecting parts of the cycle of operation. The initial complaint was about cycling, not firing the rifle.

Ruger American that they claim, "isn't loading properly."

Customer brings you a Ruger American that she claims, "isn't loading properly." Upon further questioning, you discover that she has no problem loading ammunition into the magazine, but that when she closes the bolt, it does not always grab the next round. The customer has only used one brand of ammunition that she can recall.

How to safely remove/clear the magazine, chamber, and barrel of ammunition and potential obstructions.

The Ruger American uses a detachable magazine so I would first remove the feeding source. Next, I would ensure the rifle is on safe and I would open the action by rotating the bolt and pulling it rearward to expose the chamber of the barrel. Finally, I would remove the bolt from the frame and inspect the barrel for any obstructions using a bore light.

Initial Inspection and Diagnosis

The Ruger American is a Bolt Action rifle. I do not believe it would fall into the faulty ammunition category because the issue is not to do with firing but loading specifically. It is possible the user is not pulling the bolt handle all the way to the rear when loading and the bolt face never reaches the head or rim of the round to chamber.

Test you might perform to verify the customer's complaint and why I might choose this method over others.

I would use snap caps chambered in the same caliber as the rifle in question and I would see if it stripped the top round of the magazine to properly chamber the round. I would also inspect the magazine spring to ensure the magazine is giving the proper lift to the follower to seat the next round for chambering.

Detailed Assessment

We have 2 Ruger American rifles in the rental pool at the live fire facility I currently work at. This is not common in ours because we clean and inspect our rentals regularly, but it is not to say this is not common across the board. The issue we come across the most is operator error like not disengaging the safety or not pulling the bolt handle all the way to the rear to chamber the next round.

Assuming that the component I originally suspected was not the culprit of the failure, what other component might I suspect and why?

If the ammunition and magazine are fine and the user is operating the firearm correctly then it is possible that the locking lug that is also responsible for stripping the top round from the magazine is rounded off or even broken and it is slipping over the round in the magazine.

Assuming the magazine spring was the cause of the malfunction, I will describe the type of failure, what components caused the malfunction, the components I might remove or replace, and the tests that were performed to verify operation:

After taking the time to make sure the firearm was unloaded and free of obstructions, I began trying to recreate the issue. In doing so with inert snap cap ammunition I noticed the rounds in the magazine were not being pushed upward enough to catch the part of the bolt face responsible for chambering the ammunition. This led me to believe the issue was not with the firearm but with the feeding source. I removed the magazine spring and pulled it to its appropriate length for the correct tension and this resolved the issue of feeding the ammunition. However, this is a temporary fix and a new magazine or just a new magazine spring will be needed to properly fix the issue.

SECTION FOUR:
CUSTOM WORK & ALTERATIONS

What type of holster do I use and what about that holster that works well? Would I change anything if I could?

As a firearms instructor at a live fire facility, I carry every day. I almost never carry concealed because I live in Texas, and they allow open carry. Also, on the off chance I need to use it I don't want to have to clear clothing to draw it. Almost all of the holsters I use are made with Kydex and are Blackhawk brand with level II retention. This works well for me, but I preach to my students that just because I like it does not mean that they will. To those who are just getting into carrying a firearm, I usually recommend that they wear the holster they chose for at least one week before deciding if they like it or not. This is because they are new to carrying and just about any holster will feel foreign to them and may be uncomfortable at first.

You may ask, Why Kydex? This is because it is durable and will not retain moisture like leather or nylon will. Sure, the more you draw from it, the more wear will show on the finish of the gun, but I just need a functioning firearm, not a pretty one. Why did I choose Blackhawk as my brand of choice? They are usually a little cheaper in cost than some of the other companies and speaking from experience, you will still get years of use out of them. Do I need level II retention? In Texas they do not stipulate any level of retention as a requirement but because I choose to carry openly, I prefer to have some type of retention just in case someone tries to take it from my holster. The only issue I found annoying when using this holster is the way it was worn. The two options it usually comes with are the larger paddle type that slides into the pants or the belt loop attachment. As a fix to this issue, I purchased the Blackhawk Quick Release Dial so I can remove and reattach the firearm with ease and I'm not in public messing around with my belt every time I want to remove it or put it back on.

The purpose of the retention device you are thermoforming and why I choose this one to start.

The type of retention device I decided to make for my first ever Kydex press was for an H&K VP9 magazine. Its purpose is to allow me to carry additional magazines on my waist and not just jammed into a pocket. I chose to make this in part because I did not already have one for this firearms magazine and because I did not want to waste a ton of material in the learning process and be stuck with too little Kydex to make another attempt if the first one did not turn out well.

The object I used to generate the dimensions of the design.

I used multiple objects to determine how much material to use for the press I was about to do on the H&K VP9 magazine. I started off using the magazine. By placing it directly on the raw material I was able to see how much of the magazine I wanted to stick out and this let me see how much material I wanted to use for the press. By making a general mark I now had an idea as to where I needed to measure and mark. Next, I used a square that also has Measurements marked on it. I rounded up to the nearest inch to allow myself more material than I thought I would need. It is better to have too much rather than not enough.

Challenges you may face when constructing the mold.

I did run into one issue while following the instructions provided and that was when attaching the top of the press. The text has you attach your hinges directly to the piece of 2x4 but when I did this the foam provided was way too thick to allow for closure. While I do understand that the pressure created by the foam is what aids in a good press in the mold, by following that step I found it really difficult to even close over the press. To remedy this, I took another piece of the 3/4 Inch board and cut it to the same dimensions as the 2x4 then attached it to the top of the exposed 2x4. This additional 3/4 Inch allowed me to then finish attaching my hinges and allowed a tight, but more manageable closing of the press.

What your setup might look like when creating thermoformed holsters for sale to the public.

The funny thing is that I have already started selling thermoformed holsters to the public at the live fire facility I currently work out of. Yes, someone who has just learned this type of holster making and has already bought more equipment than probably what is really needed can immediately begin selling their work and I became that guy because of the course I took. I converted an old storage room in the facility I worked at and then I had a space to begin my work as a gunsmith. It had a fair bit of counter space, but the room could have been larger as I planned on investing in some larger equipment. I have not built the confidence yet to begin offering custom press work, but I have already jumped into making and selling Kydex holsters for our most popular firearms. Once I knew that this was something I could really do I purchased equipment like a rivet press, professional steel plate press, scroll saw, belt sander and Dremel tool to make the process even easier and with these items I can work at an almost continuous rate to produce a lot of products. However, as I am an operations manager, firearms instructor, Chief RSO, gunsmith, full time student and father of 3, I cannot work at the scale I would like to. This is a way of turning a profit with an extra few minutes every day, for me and the business. Like anything else in life, the more you do something the better you get at it and investing in better tools and more materials only aids in the process of learning this new skill. Not only is this something I considered doing, but it's also something I decided to do and recommend others consider doing as well.

The process of completing a retention device and what the most challenging part was & why.

Creating a press—With any level of experience working with your hands and a basic understanding of some simple tools anyone could make a Kydex Press. I think the two most important parts of this process are the hinges you choose, and the foam material used to actually press the Kydex to the object. Hinges that are too small and made for something like a jeweler box will not last long because of the amount of pressure it takes to get a good press and cheap foam may melt to the warm Kydex or be worn out after just a few uses.

Planning your design—For some, planning your design may take two full days to get just right with exact dimensions listed Etc. I would work like this a long time ago and I found one major flaw with this type of design process and that is the expectations vs reality. Making a quick sketch and taking the extra time to prep everything every time works best for me now. I may misalign the Kydex during the press or miss a spot when drilling my holes for rivets and this results in an imperfect product. We are human and thus prone to error. In most cases it becomes how can I save this rather than the expectation of perfection.

Constructing your mold—When making the Mold or prepping the item that is going to be pressed, it is important to think this step out. Areas like the ejection port and the section in front of the trigger need to be filled in to avoid over pressing and creating undercuts that make it more difficult to use the holster. When making a taco style, one piece holster, it is important to create a channel your pistols front sight can slide in and out of. Finally, block the area you think you will mount your belt hook to and if the firearm has things like bulky tac lights or lasers attached to them, you will need to block the item out, so the holster has a channel for things like that to slide in and out of as well.

Pressing and heating your design—The process of heating and pressing the Kydex moves really fast. In most cases the Kydex material can get to the correct temp in just a couple minutes and once malleable, will only give you half that in workable time before it begins to cool off and become unusable. On average I will heat the Kydex to anything from 305-345 because any hotter than that and the material will begin to miss shape and melt to the tray I use to heat. Lastly, unless you are used to handling hot things bare handed, use some gloves when handling the heated Kydex. This not only protects but allows for a more controlled press of the material.

Finishing procedures—The finishing procedure has got to be my favorite part of this whole process. This is the step where everything starts to take shape and you begin to see the finished product. Depending on what tools you have on hand this step can also be the most tedious. If using a hack saw to trim material and sanding by hand to clean up your edges, this step may be your least favorite. However, if using a scroll saw to trim and a belt sander to clean up your edges then you are finished in a few short minutes and usually have a cleaner looking finished product.

The most challenging part of this process, why and what I might do differently next time to mitigate that challenge.

If I was asked what I thought the most challenging part of this process was I would have to say it was the design portion. One mistake in your design has ripple effects in your finished product. Forgetting to block off a section where you would be attaching belt clips could result in mounting screws scratching the firearm or magazine every time it is drawn. I really want to knock out a quick design so as to not over think the process but in reality, this is the one step where you need to stop and think out all the tiny details.

A reflection on the process of building my own kydex press for use with thermoforming.

Materials you can use to create your own press.

For this I was asked to build my own Kydex Press out of wood. So, I did just that and used 3/4In plywood and 2In x 4In wood. When it came time to pick the hinges for the top of the press, I decided to go with some smaller ones rather than gate or exterior door hinges. This kept them small enough to fit the 8In width the foam material came in. Finally, I did purchase deck screws and used them to not only assemble the base but to attach the hinge. Hinges usually come with screws that are small and using those may result in the press breaking during the process.

One type of clamping method and hinged design that keeps your mold secure while pressing the form into place.

I used smaller hinges with an odd design that has one rounded side and a spike shape to the other side. The reason I chose these was because I figured the pressure from pressing may dig in with this shape hinge rather than slide out of alignment after a few operations. I also used the deck screws to attach them to the base to ensure they don't rip out under the pressure of the press. The clamps I am using are basic Irwin Quick Grips instead of the vice style that thread tight. The reason I decided to use Quick Grips is because I want pressure fast to shape the Kydex before it begins to harden.

How durable do you believe your design will be in the long run?

I believe the wood press I made will last for some time because took into consideration the grain of the wood when measuring and cutting my pieces. I figured that if the grain of the wood was horizontal then the pressure placed on it by the clamps may eventually crack the plywood. Granted, I can't see the grain of the other pieces that layer the plywood but I still made sure that my top and bottom layers had vertical grain so the wood would more likely bend instead of crack.

Tools & materials that are needed for preparing firearms before spray on finishes.

The tools and materials needed to prep a firearm for a spray on finish may include things like acetone to degrease the parts and a sandblaster to remove any old worn coating before starting to apply a new one. The sandblaster also creates a rougher surface to allow the spray on finish to adhere better. As we are talking about hazardous materials like chemicals and fine particulate, it is important to list personal protective equipment in the required items list as well. Making sure you are not breathing in the medium used to sandblast is very important to your immediate health. Also making sure the acetone doesn't get on your bare skin is important, so chemical resistant gloves are ideal. Finally, masking tape and a bunch of different sized rubber plugs may be a good idea to prevent overspray from building up on and in parts that should not have the coating applied. If the spray on coating needs to be cured in an oven it is important you use high temp plugs made of silicone rubber.

All of the items I found were listed for sale on Amazon.com and this made finding a range of options easy to acquire. Most of the acetone listed labeled for cleaning off nail polish but work for the purposes of cleaning off grease and oil on gun parts. These acetone options range from $20 to $40 depending on the brand and how much you are buying. I would use any of these acetone options myself. When looking for sandblasters you will have a number of options ranging from $55 to $265 depending on if it is used in a blasting cabinet or used as an open-air device. The options I chose for this are reasonably priced, but you could spend a few thousand dollars for a larger cabinet allowing multiple Users at the same time. This also did not include the price of the compressor needed to begin blasting. For cost reasons I would use the open-air option with good PPE. Both options will still require the use of a respirator to avoid inhaling particulate. Even if the blasting cabinet has a ventilation option fine particulate can still escape and be inhaled. With regard to the use of barrel plugs and masking tape it is important to make sure they are heat resistant. Some spray on finishes requires they be cured in an oven of sorts and a rubber plug that melts during this process does you no good and may present a fire hazard. The high temp options I was able to find range from $28 to $35 and come in a range of sizes. I would use any of the options listed because they include the same stuff, and the cost is about the same. Finally, I went looking for personal protection kits that included things like mask, eye protection and gloves to ensure the health and safety of the individual doing the work. This can range anywhere from $14 to $30 depending on the kit and its contents. I may not purchase the kits I listed but rather spend more money on better quality equipment because my health is very important to me.

Attempt to blue or brown a gun part for a customer using a spray-on method.

The spray on bluing I found was on amazon and is made by Duracoat. Most of the spray on options I was looking at were very different than the bluing solution in the bottle that you would use on bare metal. After reading a few customer reviews on this product specifically, most loved the end result but compare it to more of an epoxy coating rather than a chemical reaction produced with the Perma Blue. I think I would talk to the customer about what they want the finished product to look like and that may help me decide how to achieve it. Of course, the decision may be a lot easier depending on the items that need bluing. If the customer wants a barrel or frame done and they like the glossy finish this Duracoat gives them, then that would be my solution but I don't think I would ever use such a solution on machine screws because it sounds like there is some build up that may result in the threading no longer working in the firearm and this would be really bad come time to reassemble the weapon system. Another reason I would not use the Duracoat on machine screws is because the screw that gets too much of this solution in the head may prevent my bit from properly seating and the buildup may cause me to slip the bit and ruin the head of the screw. It may even be that some jobs require both Perma Blue on machine screws and the Duracoat on the frame as requested by the customer. Anyway, you go about it please be sure that you follow directions and apply the solution correctly or you may make a costly mistake with a client's gun. It's a lot more work to use the Perma Blue but I feel like the result is more aesthetically pleasing so if I had the choice, that would be it.

Can you ever see yourself abandoning conversion or heat-based procedures for spray on?

If the result desired by the customer is a color, then yes, I would agree that spray on finishes is the future. However, a lot of people are getting away from the classic methods of bluing and browning type finishes which leads me to believe that I should invest in the older methods first. Anyone can buy a can of this spray on stuff and give it a shot on their own making the gunsmith obsolete. Sure, the average joe wouldn't spend the money for a full Cerakote kit with sprayer and all, but you can purchase some of this stuff in rattle cans now making it cheap and easy for anyone to give it a try. I think investing in hot bluing tanks and the chemicals and equipment needed to brown is smart and having everything needed to offer the classic finishes will always pay out because most people have no idea where to begin in that type of process and would feel it necessary to find a gunsmith who specializes in it. Would I consider offering the spray on finishes once I get my FFL up and running? Yes, but only to offer color options to customers and that is it. Being a clients one stop shop for all their gun needs is a great thing so I would offer as much type of work as possible but investing in something countless others already offer becomes competitive and I would not see the return on investment I would like. My advice is to look at your local competition and do everything they are not because once the lowest price battle begins on the same work everyone loses.

My personal reflection on the process of applying hydrographic coating.

Let me start by saying that I was skeptical at first about how the Hydro Dipping process was going to achieve such detailed finishes. After a few attempts and some trial and error using a test piece I ended up loving the finished product. I chose the standard two-piece AR-15 hand guards to dip for this project because we have a few that have sat here in the shop for some time now and if I had messed them up, it would be no harm and no foul. In my opinion anyone looking to try this themselves should first try one or two items they do not care for before attempting to dip their entire firearm.

Like anything we do it is important to read the directions thoroughly before making your first attempt. The process seems simple when reading through the provided instructions but after doing some more research on the topic I saw that many people had issues with getting their desired results. Things like too much or too little activator being applied can give the user mixed results. Also, taping all 4 sides of the film can cause issues during the dip and may result in water getting to the top of the film unintentionally.

You do want to be sure you frame up the border edge of the film to ensure it does not disperse or move when the activator is applied but I found my own solution for this.

The dip tank I decided to use for this project ended up being just a 5-gallon bucket. This gave me a large enough area for the amount of film needed for the items I was going to dip and was deep enough for me to fully submerge the items. Instead of using tape edges or a PVC frame as suggested in the instructions I marked the buckets diameter directly on the film giving me the perfect amount of film for the inside of the bucket. This essentially made the bucket I was using my frame thus ensuring my film would not disperse or drift away. I would tell others looking to try this technique to find a way to frame the film without tape. The edges do roll up a little, but this only helps ensure that water does not reach the surface.

My first real attempt at this did show one or two spots that blemished a bit. I believe this was because after the dipping process you need to wash off the slimy residue that is left on the product and I think I missed those areas. I was worried that if I scrubbed it too hard the pattern would begin to rub off. This will happen if being too rough with the cleaning process so take the time to rinse off the item that was dipped. I had not noticed the spots until applying the clear coat but once the clear coat began reacting with the spots, it became noticeable. All in all, I felt like this was a rather simple process that yielded some amazing results, and I would definitely consider offering this service in the future.

The process of case hardening a firearm and modern chemical methods of case hardening.

Admittedly at the start of this I had no idea how this was achieved but I had seen it a number of times while working for a few different live fire facilities. This is the process of adding carbon to low carbon steel creating a hard outer shell while leaving the inside tough but malleable. Doing this adds durability to the firearm but not so much as to make the entire steel component brittle and vulnerable to breaking. Animal bones were used back in the day to achieve this but today most use Bone Charcoal as their carbon element. When correctly heated the bone element converts to a carbon rich gas that bonds to the low carbon steel surface creating a denser carbon steel shell. The longer it is held at temperature the deeper the carbon will penetrate the low carbon steel you started with. Once you're done heating it to the desired level of density the items are taken out of the furnace and quenched with water and oil to rapidly cool the items and get that iconic multi color look to the steel. Please don't forget to clean and oil the items after you are done and they have cooled off because if not you may come back to find those beautiful items covered in rust. This is something probably best learned with time and lots of practice but if you know someone who can get the result, I found with this quick google search it may be beneficial to pick their brain a little.

The advantages and risks of offering "jeweling" services at a gunsmith's shop.

Well, I can say I had fun looking this one up and yes, I do believe it is worth spending the money to add this service to my shop. Now, like anything else you do it is worth spending a little more up front to get the right equipment for the job. I was able to find things like the Wheeler brand Jeweling fixture that was incredibly cheap and selling for around $35 for the fixture but it had some pretty bad reviews. However, after watching a few Midway USA videos on YouTube I noticed they were using the Indexing Spin Jigs 5C Drilling Mill Lathe Grinding Collet 5C Fixture Drill. This tool runs at about $90 depending on where you look and is a much better tool that is built to last a lifetime of work. After that I found a deluxe jeweling kit on Brownell's for another $90 and this came with the abrasive rods and other componence to do the job right. Add to the cost the sandpaper needed to prep the surface and you only invested about $200 to do some amazing work. Please note this did not include the cost of the drill press used to do the work but if you're like me this may be something already in your inventory of tools. I don't think everyone with a bolt action rifle is looking to have this work done but the ones who do understand the value, craftsmanship and style this brings to a well finished rifle.

SECTION FIVE:
TIPS FOR A BETTER SHOOTING FIREARM

There is an old adage that shooters should always purchase the best scope they can afford, but should they?

Because of my experience helping shooters with their telescoping sights, I would say you don't always need the best optics on the market. You should be purchasing what is best suited for the caliber of firearm you are mounting it to. Crimson Trace and Leopold make outstanding scopes, but I wouldn't be mounting one meant for a rim fire to my 300 WIN MAG. Knowing the ballistics of the caliber I'm shooting and what optic best suits my caliber is probably the best way to go about this. Now with that being said, I recommend you do not buy scopes with tons of features you have no understanding of. If looking through your scope feels like a laser guidance system on an F-22 Raptor and you have no idea what you're looking at, then it may be time to start leaning the features or switching to a simple reticle you can understand.

I have always offered a zeroing service at the range for those who have no idea how to go about doing this. I keep it relatively cheap and can usually get it done in the first 10 rounds. This means that I too have used a few scopes I had no real understanding of. Thermal scopes have become popular here in Texas because of coyote and hog problems and these can be relatively easy if you know what you're doing. I have shot thermal that ranges in price from $4,000 to $14,000 and if I'm being totally honest, there was not a ton different between the two systems. I have zeroed telescoping sights on anything from a Barret to a Ruger 10/22 and when the appropriate sight is mounted to the firearm it zeros well and holds true for a long time. My advice, buy cheap buy twice so don't buy junk. However, you should not need to spend more on the sight than you did with the firearm.

Illustrating my definition of accuracy by describing scenarios and experiences.

For this I will be speaking from my own perspectives and experiences regarding accuracy. Currently I am a licensed instructor in four states and work for a live fire facility outside of Ft Hood Texas. I fell into this line of work because I had an old friend ask for my help to train different police departments back in Baltimore where I am from originally. Now having done this for some time, let's talk about my definition of accuracy.

I believe accuracy to be one's ability to hit an intended target despite the many factors that can hinder them, but I also believe accuracy to be the firearms ability to properly twist and propel a projectile toward its intended target. If the person using the firearm doesn't know some basic fundamentals of shooting, they will likely not be very accurate. If the firearm is in bad shape and the barrels rifling is worn out or damaged, you may have an accurate shooter become less effective. It's a symbiosis in the sense that to get the best possible shot, both human factors and machining need to be at their best condition. I have seen some of the best shooters shoot like junk because of poorly kept firearms and I have seen some of the best firearms miss their intended target because of the operator's inability to use it correctly. This sad fact is probably the reason people like me stay employed.

Describing the AK-47 and the method a shooter would use to adjust for accuracy at distance.

More times than not the intended purpose of the AK-47 is combat. Though individual owners in countries that are not experiencing war tend to use them for target practice, of the millions upon millions made by different countries and manufacturers, most end up in the hands of fighters around the world. This is because the piston driven system makes this firearm work in just about any environment imaginable.

The Iron Sights on the AK-47 are very well suited for this firearm. The front sight usually has a loop of metal to protect the front sight post from damage or unintended manipulation. The rear tangent iron sight usually uses a square notch that has no windage adjustment. Both windage and elevation can be adjusted on the front sight post. With this being said, I do prefer iron sights over any type of red dot or telescoping sight. The reason for this is because your iron sights can't run out of battery and have no glass lens to break.

Most AK-47's are relatively easy to adjust for distance shooting. The front sight is adjustable, and this is how you would adjust the windage and elevation. Once the front sight on an AK-47 is set to zero with the rear, you would use the rear iron sights slide bar to raise and drop the tangent sight to account for the distance being fired. Adjusting for distance doesn't require any additional tools.

Accurizing a Remington Model 700 that has little success at ranges beyond one hundred yards.

Let us say a customer brings you a Remington 700 with a Vortex Viper HS LR Scope mounted on it and wants you to make it more accurate. The customer mentions that they have had little success hitting targets beyond one hundred yards but wants to go on a hunt where they will need to hit 200 plus yards. How would someone go about doing this? Well, one of the first things I would like to do is get this person on a rifle I already know is capable of achieving this task. My purpose for this is to see if the shooter has the ability or knowledge to operate at those distances. If so, then it may be time to start looking at the rifle.

After a quick inspection of the rifle, making sure it is safe to operate, I will confirm zero and test fire it to see if the scope or rifle have any noticeable issues that are easy to correct. It's possible that the scope just wasn't zeroed correctly in the first place. The next thing I will be inspecting is the barrel and muzzle. Damage to the muzzle can affect accuracy so if I see any noticeable issues there then I would consider fixing the barrel's crown. Now that I'm satisfied there, I'll begin to inspect the rest of the barrel. Using a bore scope, I will look for damage to the rifling and see if there was any copper fouling that may be affecting accuracy. If copper or nitro fouling were the issue, I would use Birchwood Casey Bore Scrubber in the barrel to start the cleaning process followed with the appropriate patches, jags, and bore brushes to finish cleaning out the existing rifling.

If the crown on the barrel is chipped my next steps may vary depending on where it is and how deep it is. If it is chipped where the rifling ends, then I may just use a brass crowning tool and some fine grit compound to lap the barrel at the muzzle until I have worked it out. Otherwise, if the chip is deeper and not at the rifling's end, I may use a 45-degree crowning tool to clean up the center of the crown or an 11-degree crowning tool to clean up the entirety of the muzzle. It is also possible that I may need to remove a small section of the barrel at the muzzle end.

Taking a look at the bore now, I begin to look for cleanliness and possible rust, especially rust pitting where it had sat for so long that it began to eat into the metal. This is important anywhere on the barrel, but it matters most at the bore because that is the spot that has to take most of the pressure when a cartridge is fired. If the rust pitting is bad enough, I would usually recommend that the customer purchase a new one and have it installed for safety reasons. I have had to tell one or two people in the past that their options were a new barrel or cleaning it up and making it wall art, never to be fired again. Usually when they look at the options, they decide to get a new barrel, and this is when it is important to inspect the lock up of the bolt lugs to the chamber. The same receiver's shoulders have similar wear to the existing bolt lugs, and they work fine but when a new barrel is installed, they may need to be worked in a little to ensure the lugs meet the chamber recesses.

By starting a process called blueprinting, you ensure the barrel is true to the receiver and that the locking lugs are true to the barrel. In doing this I will also need to make sure the recoil lug is perfectly flat on both sides. Truing up the Bolt surfaces may help it lock up to the new barrels chamber by ensuring it has full contact with the shoulders in the receiver and this should then aid in making the rifle more accurate. One useful technique when lapping Remington action is using a bolt lug lapping tool, action bushings, a piloted reamer, a piloted tap, and bolt face cutters with a guide to be sure everything has cleaned new surfaces for better lock up. If you wish to see how to use those tools to properly achieve the action lapping, YouTube has a few videos with my favorite being by Larry Potterfield and Midway USA.

Explaining the process for lapping and breaking in the bore and how "fire Lapping" works.

If the rifle does not have a new barrel, the process for lapping and breaking in the bore may be done like this.

Before I start the process of lapping or breaking in a barrel, especially one that is not new, I will take a bore scope to the barrel and inspect the lands and grooves for damage, rusting or pitting. It is possible that the barrel is beyond repair and that a new barrel is the only real solution to fixing the issue. If I have determined that lapping may fix the issue and not just a quick cleaning, then I may decide to lap the bore or even fire lap the barrel. This may clean up some of the barrel's issues and make for better spin on the round and give the individual user a better shot group at distance.

Nathan Foster, the author of the practical guide to bolt action accurizing and maintenance, mentions bringing a wide range of things to the range when breaking in a rifles barrel. These items include things like cleaning rods, bronze brushes, copper solvent, degreaser, 4x2 patches, and Autosol. He goes on to say that many copper solvents are "Truly, utterly useless, pointless liquids." And that "You would be better off taking leak down the bore." (Foster, 2014, page 85) A good way to see if your copper cleaner works well is to try some on a copper FMJ and to look for a reaction. The solution should breakdown the copper and it should have an etched look if it works well. Cleaning the rifles barrel is important and copper fouling can cause accuracy issues. A good copper solvent may solve the problem. So, let's cover hand lapping the bore and why it is important. For new rifles this may remove factory burrs and improve the finish but with older rifles this can be considered part of your barrel's regular maintenance. By taking a bronze brush and a maroon-colored poly pad you can lap the throat section of the barrel by running these back and forth inside the first three inches of the barrel. This helps remove some of the factory machining marks. Next you will repeat the process in the rest of the barrel stopping at about three inches from the muzzle. Nathan Foster says you should "get in there and give that barrel a good kick in the pants." (Foster, 2014, page 89) This means you should really work this section and not worry about damaging the rifle. Finally, you want to work the muzzle end but, in a careful, controlled manner. Allow the brush to exit the muzzle a little bit but do not totally remove it with each stroke. Only 8-10 strokes are recommended. Then you can use the Autosol he mentions on the worn pad to run through the barrel again to try and get a clean finish to the inside of the barrel.

"Fire lapping" and the purpose of this procedure.

Some people would prefer to work the barrel using a method called fire lapping, but Nathan Foster says this should be considered a last resort. Fire lapping is the process of adding a cutting grit to the projectile and firing it through the barrel in an effort to fix any issues the barrels lands may have. A burr halfway down a barrel is going to affect the projectile and make for a less accurate shot. Doing this may also correct any abnormal bore dimensions and give you a consistent grip and twist on the projectile. This takes time if you do it correctly so be sure not to rush this process. One approach is to start with a 220-grit on five rounds and clean the barrel after every shot. This prevents buildup and allows each bullet to do its job. Then, even though Nathan Foster doesn't recommend it, move to a 320-grit compound, and fire another five rounds again cleaning the barrel after every shot. Finally use a much finer 600-grit compound on the projectiles and fire your last five rounds again cleaning the barrel after each shot. If you decide not to clean the other grits out as you fire, then you may expect mixed results as the grits build up and mix.

Scope sizes, adjustability and an introduction to what Parallax is when shooting.

A 50 mm objective lens is preferable to a smaller lens when the shooter needs a wide field of view. In combat I may need to see what is going on in a wide range of areas and a 50mm objective lens helps me achieve that. Using a smaller lens may help me focus on one specific target but without that wider field of view I may not have seen the innocent person crossing into my bullets flight path until it is too late. If I were just target shooting, the wider field of view a 50mm lens gives me may not be needed because I am not worried about what the shooter next to me is hitting.

The size of a scope tube has more to do with adjustability than light-allowance because the size of the scope tube has nothing to do with the amount of light that is allowed. In fact, the reason you may want a larger scope tube would be to have the ability to make more adjustments or have more travel in the erector assembly. If I know I'm doing some long-range shooting and the caliber of bullet I'm firing has significant drop at distance, I may want a larger scope tube so I can make a larger adjustment in elevation when firing.

Now most telescoping optics have a degree of parallax when looking through the lens at a target. For those who do not know what parallax is, it is when the object you are looking at appears to move or change position as the shooter's point of view changes. Motion parallax can be perceived as an object or cross hairs moving as the shooter moves their head or eye position to adjust for a shot. This type of motion parallax is more noticeable in higher magnification scopes.

The procedure you should follow when mounting, aligning, and lapping the scope rings.

For this, I will discuss in short, the procedure I followed to mount, align, and lap the scope rings for my AR-15 scope mounting project. To start mounting the rings to the picatinny rail already provided on the upper receiver of the AR-15 platform was as simple as tightening down a few retention screws after the rings were placed in position for the West Hunter scope I was mounting. Then I place the alignment pins in the rings and look to see if they are off and, in most cases, they are by a little bit. Then I applied the lapping compound, laid in the lapping bar, and worked it back and forth making minor adjustments in tightness as I went. If you took your time and did this correctly when you clean the lapping compound off, you should see the original black finish has been sanded away and now your alignment pins line up perfectly. Then it's off to mount and zero the new optic.

If the rings are mounted to a specific base and then lapped, those rings are now in alignment with each other and the rifle to which it was mounted. However, if something as simple as tightening, loosening, or moving one of the scope rings occurs then everything may fall out of alignment even if just by a little bit. This means that if the already lapped scope rings are removed and put onto another platform, you may need to rework the rings or even better use new ones. You want to be sure that you don't overwork the rings where they no longer hold the scope tight enough.

If a customer would like me to mount a scope and rings to their rifle, I would usually ask how they would like that done. By offering more than one type of service the customer has the option based on things like budget or specific need. Your precision shooters usually ask for the total package to include the lapping of the scope rings where your indoor 25yd range shooters don't need this step because they only ever fire at distances too close for lapped or unlapped rings to matter. The only time I would recommend not lapping the rings at all is when I place my alignment pins and they are already perfectly in line. As far as what other services I can offer the customer, doing the majority of my gunsmith work at a live fire facility, I would usually then offer a zeroing service once the scope and rings have been mounted. Being able to hand back a ready to use firearm for the customer is always a good feeling because I know the quality of work that went into achieving that for them.

Do I see enough added value from aligning and lapping a scope to include that process?

Now that I understand the importance of lapping and the difference it can make when mounting an optic, I will definitely complete this process on more of my own in the future. As a matter of fact, the AR-15 I used to complete this project was one of my own so I guess you can say I have already started doing this to some of my firearms. Now regarding my position on offering this service at the facility where I currently work, I do see the added value and would consider offering this service to customers. The question becomes, what customers understand the importance of this and are willing to pay the added cost of having this done. Some customers just want to toss an optic on so they can go shoot and have no clue what lapping is and why they would want it done. Anyone willing to have a conversation about the process of lapping scope rings and figuring out if they can or even should do this may begin to understand why they may want to do it or at least know why they cannot in some cases. In any case, it is smart business practice to be able to offer multiple different ways to complete the work. Telling the customer, I'll charge $15 to slap the optic on and $20 to zero it but then offering a full service job and saying for $X I will mount your rings, check center and lap them if needed, install your optic and ensure level, and zero it for you lets the customer know that the time it is taking to complete the work and the quality of work being done is vastly different then the quick slap it on and here you go type work you see a lot of.

SECTION SIX:
WOOD WORKING TECHNIQUES & TOOLS

A rifle's purpose, caliber, and recoil.

There are three major factors to consider when looking to purchase a new rifle or designing a stock for one and they are the rifle's purpose, the caliber it fires, and the amount of felt recoil the user gets when using it. Let us begin with the reason the rifle is being purchased. People may buy a rifle for any number of reasons, but I would say the most common would be for hunting, recreational shooting or simply because it looks cool and will impress others. Hunters want an accurate rifle that can stock the meat freezer in the most humane way possible. Recreational shooters usually purchase rifles that are a joy to fire but do not usually use them for hunting purposes. And finally, you have the "it looks cool" buyer who may or may not intend to fire this rifle at all but had to own it because "I mean look at it!" While having been employed at a gun range for several years, I have met all three types. When designing a stock, the person's intent could change your design drastically.

Usually, the hunter wants a degree of comfort while the "it looks cool" buyer wants just that, something that looks amazing regardless of comfort.

Next, we will cover the rifles caliber and tie in the amount of felt recoil it produces. While I feel like it is common sense that a 22lr has less recoil than a 300 Winchester magnum, it is important to note that not everyone knows what that means. I work at a live fire facility full-time, and I cannot even begin to explain the lack of knowledge the average person has regarding this subject. Usually by showing the customer the size difference between caliber and cost per cartridge they decide rather quickly to start with a smaller caliber. This choice is usually a smart one because the amount of felt recoil usually determines how much the user likes the firearm.

While it is true that some recreational shooters enjoy the pain that comes with repeated shots from ridiculous calibers, most people want a smooth shooting firearm. When designing a stock for either the 22lr or the 300 Winchester Magnum, it is more important to engineer the size, shape and feel of the larger calibers because a bad pitch or drop at heel on a rifle that fries 22lr wont usually equal an uncomfortable or painful shot.

Factors to consider before starting a gunstock project.

To start a hypothetical gunstock project, I would need to select a type of wood that is durable by looking for one that has a tight good-looking grain to it. So, I may go with the popular choice of many and use a walnut. I chose this wood because walnut is known for its strength, stability, and attractive grain patterns and there are many types to choose from so this choice still allows me to shop around a bit. Also, walnut can be relatively easy to work with, allowing me to create some intricate designs and shaping without excessive effort. Finally, this type of wood can be resistant to shock and wear, which are important qualities for any gunstock.

As far as the finish I would decide to use for this stock, I think I have decided on using an epoxy type of finish. This choice was made for a few reasons but mainly because it is one medium I have some experience with. This type of finish is a resin type coating that provides a moisture resistant, super-hard finish and gives the stock and its grain a high gloss finish. I have been known to be rough with some of my firearms and this beautiful finish is hard enough to help protect my stock from the abuse I will likely do to it. I understand it is not unbreakable, but this does give me the best chance at longevity. I would say that the only downside to my finish being epoxy it that it can take a while to get applied and dried compared to other finishes and that checkering is out of the question unless using power tools, but this is the sacrifice I have decided to make.

Building a new rifle stock while considering a limited budget and skill level.

Consider that I just got started building a new rifle stock and I have a very limited budget and skill level; I may need to think of a few things I can do to save money but still get decent results. The first thing I would hope most people would consider when just starting off is the amount of time and attention to detail necessary to complete this task correctly. Putting tools and costs aside for the moment, this type of work will take some time and if not done correctly then you will need to start over and eat the cost of your mistakes. However, since we are on the topic of mistakes, it is important to note that if this is your first time ever working on a new stock then it is okay to make mistakes. It can be part of the learning process, but it may be smart to practice a few times before offering a customer base this type of service.

So, let's work on a budget and say that I cannot find any inletting black or that it is just too expensive. Well, I can achieve the same result using a mix of lamp black oil paint and petroleum jelly, both of which I already have because I am a father of three. Next you could use T-handle screws which I do recommend but it is important that when you use them, you do not crank them too tightly as it could damage the stock and result in false readings. Thinking about the budget again, I would probably just use the screws that come with the rifle. Not ideal but remember, I am being cheap. I do think barrel inletting tools, chisels, and gouges are important for a great fit so I may splurge and get a good set of those but to wrap up my work it would probably be on the cheap again and I would likely just use a few grits of sandpaper for shaping and a smooth finish.

Basic wood working tools.

Think of this as an overview of the basic woodworking tools you would need to begin your own gunstock wood working customization project. Please note that the tools being discussed are just the basics and not a comprehensive list of items you must have to complete your project. For example, a butter knife would not be listed as a basic woodworking tool but if you find a use for it that works well for the project you are working on then so be it.

To begin, a decent set of wood rasps is a great place to start. Not to be confused with metal files, which look very similar, wood rasps give you a very rough cut on the wood and should only be used when shaping the wood into a gun stock. Next, we have curved tooth files that again work well to shape the wood particularly for your final contouring of combs, grip areas and more. Another few tools to consider are the cabinet rasp, which are less course than standard wood rasp, pattern makers rasps, which is usually used once the basic shape is achieved and you want a smoother finish, and the horse rasps that are usually much thinner and fine toothed.

Finally, we will discuss the 4-in-1 hand rasps file. This type of file gives the user four very different types of rasps in the same tool. This tool has a rasp and file section on a flat side and the same on the other, but the other side has a half round shape. This all-in-one type of file may be a great place to start when buying tools for this type of work and is currently a staple in most stock makers' basic tool collection.

Three major types of stock carving techniques.

The three major types of carving techniques are single line, low relief, and high relief. Single line carving is primarily used for things like checkering work and other intricate patterns as they are formed using a bunch of individual lines cut close together. Low Relief carving is deeper cuts made into the surface of the stock leaving untouched sections looking as though it is raised when it is not. This type of carving gives off a 3D effect when observed. Finally, we have high relief carvings. High relief carvings are not usually done to stocks that already have their shape cut as you would need to find a way to add wood for this effect. Usually when you are shaping the stock yourself, you would leave a few raised sections where you plan to do this type of work. This ensures the raised sections really stand out and are still a solid part of the actual stock.

As a kid who went to boy scouts for a brief period, I remember using punch tools on leather to create cool looking designs. As an adult, I went to school for Glass Art because I had a background in glass blowing. Now as a gunsmith, I have found a way to be creative and make art using the wood of a gun stock. Even if I didn't offer this service to a customer base, I feel like I would enjoy learning all three types of wood carving during my career as I tend to lean toward the creative artistic side of things. If this in not like you than this would feel more like work than fun.

The intricacies of custom checkering.

This discussion we will discuss the intricacies of custom checkering and decide if we would use a traditional pattern or a custom one. To be honest, I had no idea what I wanted to do so I waited to see what others were deciding when I was completing this work with SDI. I wanted to see where that took me. So down the rabbit hole I went, and I had decided to do a custom pattern. Like anything I am trying for the first time, my thoughts outshine my ability.

One of the main reason I had decided to do something custom is because I was on some forum when someone chimed in by saying that every checkering job is a custom one because of the type and shape of the stock. This made a lot of since to me as the decal provided this week may fit some stocks and not others. This being said, my personality type has never been one to keep on a straight line but one who enjoys the path less taken. Also, I figured that if I can create something hard that looks well done, then when I am asked to do the easy stuff, it should feel even easier to me. What I still need to work out in my head is the what and the how. I wanted to incorporate a shape or image of something but had been undecided on whether to fill in one large shape or image with checkering or if I wanted the shape or image to be surrounded by the checkering.

The plan for the pattern you should be completing for your first ever attempt at checkering should be simple and by the book. Lay the decal on the wood and use a pinpoint to mark the corners, edges, and master lines. Then remove the paper decal and play connect the dots using a straight edge and a pencil. I have found that by using a measuring tape you can lay it on curved sections unlike using a ruler. You can then use a knife to follow the drawn lines, then a single line cutter to follow the knife cuts. Your first cuts using the checkering tool will be slow with short strokes but once you have a well-established line, you should use slow long draws with the tool until all my border and master lines are complete.

Checkering does, in fact, take a lot of time to do and even longer to master. Sure, there are tools like power checkers that can speed up the work some but making a mistake with a tool like this usually means irreputable damage or a complete restart of the work so mastering this type of work is still important.

I think the amount of checkering work you will receive is dependent on how you market your ability to do the work and the results you produce looking good. I do not believe that word of mouth would be enough, at least at first, to fill your shop with this type of work. However, knowing how to market and doing things like creating a website to promote and book work can absolutely begin to bring in more work and now it can come from all over the country or even the world.

I think that how you spend your time is very important, but I view this a little differently than others. Having fought in a foreign country I can say that you should enjoy what time you do have in this world. At best you have 80 summers, eighty springs, 80 winters etc. and the first 20 and your last 10 your limited in your ability to accomplish task so that means at best you have 50 years of doing something you want to. If that is checkering gun stocks, then get after it but if it's something else than focus on that. In other words, find the task and build the skills you enjoy most and with enough work and determination you can become some of the best out there.

Securing the stock without a cradle.

For my first project I did not create a cradle for the stock for one reason. I started working with a raw piece of wood and not an already shaped stock. Tossing a finished stock into a regular vice can damage the wood and is not recommended. However, because I really did not see myself turning this hunk of wood into a finished product, I was not too worried if the vice left a few marks. If I decide to continue practicing hand checkering, then I would absolutely make or purchase a cradle to work the wood.

So let us talk a little bit about how a cradle is made and some of the advantages of using one. The cradle is a very useful tool designed to hold the stock in one position so the individual working the wood can focus on the checkering and not how to hold the dang thing. Cradles are just a few pieces of wood that bolt into one another and allow a secure fit for a rifle or shotgun stock. The foregrip end may have a PVC pipe cap or something similar allowing stocks of different shapes and thickness to be held. This is tightened down using a threaded rod and a wing nut. The other end, also known as the butt holder, also uses a threaded rod and a wing nut to hold the butt end of the stock in place. Both front and rear rods come through an L shaped cut of wood that is secured on both ends of a long cut of wood. Using a dowl in one hole and a bolt, nut, and washer through the other so you can adjust the placement up and down the long piece. You may just be working with a short butt stock piece or a longer one piece for something like a muzzle loader.

Preparing a wood blank before checkering.

To be 100% honest, I have always thought that the shaping and finishing of a stock was hard. Now to be clear, my work is far from perfect, but I have always stayed clear of this kind of work worrying that I might mess something up. The procedure I followed was basic.

First, I took the block of wood and in a vice began sanding, working from an 80-grit paper all the way up to a 600-grit paper. Next, I used a Tact Cloth to remove any dust and I repositioned the wood in the vice. From there I used MINWAX Gunstock 231 and a staining sponge and applied one coat to the smooth sections and let dry for 5 hours, though the can said 4 hours was fine. Finally, I applied MINWAX Tung oil, let sit for ten minutes and buffed it into the wood as instructed. Wait 24 hours, apply another coat of Tun Oil, waited another 24 hours and then I was ready to lay down my checkering pattern.

Checkering the wood before you apply any type of stain or varnish can be a bad idea for a few reasons. Based on some of the things I see online this can be tricky and ill-advised because you just created a ton of different channels on the wood by checkering and when applying stain, it can pool up in the checkering leaving a darker stain than the rest of the stock. Another reason this could be a bad idea is because once a varnish is applied it can also fill the checkering design and this takes away from the grip one wants to feel when using a firearm with a checkered stock.

I think that if someone brought me a gunstock instead of a wood blank, I would probably consider offering a full-service job where I remove any stain or varnish from the wood and work from the ground up. Sure, if the customer just wants me to checker his beat-up old stock, I would because its business. However, I believe that if you could show them what kind of finished product comes from doing this then they may opt for you to do the full job. Besides, matching a stain and finish can be hard and the customer may not like the result even if the checkering was done right.

Are your checkering tools quality or not?

The checkering tools sent to me by the school were, in fact, easy to use. The longer row of teeth and angle they are set made both the short and long strokes a breeze. Seeing that this set came with the handle that is capable of interchanging multiple type checkering heads was, at first, impressive. The ease of storing the items in the kit was impressive considering each cutter did not have a handle associated with it, so its compact size was nice. Overall, this was a good tool for checkering work.

However, the interchanging checkering heads that I had originally thought so highly of, quickly became a problem. Both cutters that came with the kit broke after one or two changes and this is why. The tool comes with an Allen wrench because to mount the different heads, you must tighten down two screws to tension the bit after inserting a tiny pin through the side. Each bit has a very thin backing of metal behind the cutters with a hole drilled through for the pin to pass through. When tightening the screws to tension the cutter head, it is important you do not use much force at all as the cutter bit will break at the hole and no longer mount into the handle. Thankfully, I was done most of the checkering work when the bits broke but replacing them would not be cheap.

If anyone is thinking about starting this type of work in the future, then budget in a good set of cutters that have cutter heads dedicated to their own handles. Sure, you lose the compact size of the original kit but knowing that your cutter tips are permanently fixed and not made with thin breakable metal is worth the space you sacrifice. To be honest, there are a ton of good-looking checkering tools out there, but I don't know that I will be adding any of them to my toolbox any time soon. I had a lot of fun completing this type of work and maybe at some point I will decide to purchase them and practice some more but right now there is no budget and no real need for them today.

Summarizing the checkering process.

Whether you start with an unfinished block of wood or a pre-formed raw wood stock, the process takes time. When starting with a block of wood, you must get the shape cut and formed before you can move on to the next step and getting this done right takes work and time. Next you want to sand the wood to get a smooth finish that will accept the stain and not show defects. Once the stain and oil finish process begin, you need to allow the proper amount of time to allow the color and finish to seal correctly. This can mean 24 hours between coats and this part of the process can take the most time to get done correctly. Now you can start the process of checkering which, if done right, also takes time to do correctly. Remember, getting the border and master lines done right usually means a nice clean looking finished product once filled in.

Checkering in general can be difficult to achieve but to me the most difficult part would have to be meeting the filler lines with the boarder lines. This was made even more difficult because while completing the boarder and master lines, the cheap tools provided by the school broke right where they connected to the adjustable handle. I would honestly have to say that the one thing that would make this type of work easier in the future is a better-quality tool. Having the right tool for the job is always going to yield the best results

The declining popularity of hand checkering.

I believe one factor that is contributing to the declining popularity of hand checkering is simply technology. Back when people first started doing this type of work things like laser engravers did not exist. Checkering by hand is subject to mistakes because we are human, and a slip of the wrist can spell disaster while the use of a laser engraver can be as simple as inputting the design and hitting start.

I think gunsmiths should continue this type of gun stock art (by hand) because repair work may still be necessary even if the original work was done by a laser engraver. If checkering is damaged and you wish to fix it using a laser engraver, then you cannot just work over the existing damaged pattern. You would need to remove the finish and sand away all the original work to recreate the pattern. A finish that shines like an epoxy finish is a real issue when using a laser engraver to create a checkering pattern. Most people think that if you change the intensity of the laser then it should work through the finish and hit the wood but what you may not know is that a finish of this type can refract the laser and damage not only the stock but possibly the machine itself. I think all gunsmiths should learn checkering by hand even if it is not their area of expertise. Sure, if the customer is starting with a blank stock and wishes to have a very intricate design worked into it by hand, then they may want to find a specialist but minor repair to existing work should be available by your average gunsmith in my opinion.

Choosing a type of wood for a custom stock build.

If I were the customer and wanted to choose a type of wood for a build I am completing, I would need to explain to "the custom stock maker" why I believe this choice works for my build. So, If I were to choose a type of wood for my next project it would probably be black walnut. Not only is it still popular in a lot of gun stock builds here in America, making it appealing to the buyer, but I chose black walnut for a number of other reasons as well. This type of wood is light weight and easy to work with. This makes for a lighter overall weight for my completed build and makes the work of "the custom stock maker" a little easier. Black walnut also has a rich dark color and takes a "superior polish" thus making for an amazing finish to this project. The ease of working this type of wood is also a benefit to me because if I were to get it back from the stock maker and need to make any changes to the size, shape, or design, then I should be able to make those changes myself and not have to return to "the custom stock maker" for more work that can end up costing me more and eating into my profit margins. If this is the case and I did indeed need to make changes to the stock, then I will likely need to redo the polish when I'm done, and this type of wood holds a nice polish if done correctly.

Critical measurements when custom making a gun stock.

Knowing the critical measurements when custom making a gun stock is critical to the fitment of the gun to its user and to the overall success of your build. Things like pitch, drop at heel, length of trigger pull and the drop at comb will all make or break your sale when it comes to custom work. So, let us begin at the length of pull. The reading mentions that most American firearms have approximately a 14-inch measurement because this feels good to the average sized male, but it continues to say that taller men would prefer a longer option. The correct amount of pull should fit to the shoulder easily and allow the shooter to hook their finger around the trigger with ease. Next, we have the stocks pitch. This is essentially the flat cut that contacts the shoulder when firing. Getting this wrong could equal some pain to the user depending on body type and caliber being fired. This is easy to measure in most cases. Simply place the stock butt first on the ground and place it up against a wall, then just measure the distance the muzzle end is from the wall.

To finish up we still have the drop at heel and the drop at comb. The heel on the stock is where the top of the stock meets the butt end while the comb is located usually where the cut begins to drop again for the grip section of the stock. These measurements are alike in that they are both necessary to get the rifle's line of sight to the user's eye level. Find where the line of sight is going to be on the firearm, and you can begin to measure from there down to the comb or the heel of the stock.

Building your fundamental understanding of Inletting as a skillset.

The term inletting is used to describe the process of carefully cutting away sections of a stock to fit the receiver, barrel, and action. Typically, if you are buying a kit today there is a semi-finished stock included that has its general shape already formed and the section where you drop in your receiver, action or barrel are usually precut and only need a little work to fully complete. Using inletting black or simply by smoking the parts, press them in place and it should then mark the high spots that need trimming for proper fitment. Do this as many times as needed to get the correct fit then finish your build.

Now, it is important that you complete all metal work, minus a bluing type of finish, before performing the inletting process. Simply put, if the stock is altered to perfectly fit your metal parts and I do something like changing the contour of the barrel, then the inletting job I just did will have been for nothing. When the wood for the stock has been cut to within about 1/16th" of its final dimension, the person making the stock should begin working a lot slower making frequent checks for high spots and making the smallest adjustments possible. This is when smoking the metal parts or using inletting black becomes critical for identifying touch points that need adjusting for the best fit.

No matter the wood you have chosen to use, it is important that the grain of the wood is straight near the small end of the stock because it is known to be one of the weakest spots in your build. From butt to just before the grip you can run with whatever grain pattern you want because that section does not see the same stress as the other section does and is much thicker and durable anyway. But the small end and the grip see much more stress and are far thinner, so the grain here needs to be straight to ensure some durability.

When working a stock and you realize there is some twisting happening, you should take steps to correct it as early as possible. Using inletting black and fitting the parts, twist the stock straight. This will not correct the twist but will however show heavier markings where you need to cut and by making those cuts the stock should start to straighten out. Finally, a ton of bolt action rifles have a projection underneath the barrel. This section found just in front of the magazine well helps ensure the receiver and barrel mount snug to the wood stock. This is important because failing to fit this to the stock shoulder correctly could mean the force of the rifle being fired pushes back and could break the stock near the grip. To be honest, the actual shape of your stock can be ugly so long as this fit is done correctly. I will always prefer ugly and functional over pretty and weak.

Considering options to reduce felt recoil.

For this I have selected the Barrett M82A1 .50 Caliber rifle because it is one of the heaviest recoiling rifles on the market today. This is not often seen by many gunsmiths because of its price and availability but I have had the pleasure of working with and handling this rifle a few times myself. While I believe this rifle specifically should have every available option installed in an attempt to reduce its felt recoil, the option I would likely start with would probably be to add a suppressor to the muzzle break. The large caliber round fired by the Barrett M82A1 requires a lot of force to push the projectile out of the barrel and toward its intended target and that equals a lot of recoil.

It is important to remember that for every action there is an equal and opposite reaction so the amount of gas that is expanding through the barrel and exiting behind the round is also pushing back toward the shooter. To put this caliber into perspective, the Barrett M82A1 can retain about 1,300 foot-pounds of energy after around 2,000 yards of travel so the felt recoil on the shooter is substantial. Attaching a suppressor can greatly reduce the firearms recoil by capturing and slowing down the gasses that exit the muzzle after the shot. While this option does only further increase the overall length and weight of the rifle, its ability to slow down and capture these gases should aid in reducing felt recoil a bit and has the added benefit of reducing noise to this ridiculously loud firearm.

Rifle butt plate purposes and products.

Obviously, the preferred material used when making a rifles buttplate can be a matter of opinion. While the maker of the buttplate may like one material because it is easier to use and work with, the other person making a rifles buttplate may like another material because even though it may be harder to work with, they believe it produces a better product. Personally, I like a metal buttplate because of its durability and ease of cleaning but, as I stated before, this can be subjective because if I am choosing with comfort in mind, I may decide to use some type of foam rubber to help manage the firearms felt recoil.

Now if you are like me you may want to consider something like an adjustable buttplate. What feels right for me today may feel off to me tomorrow and having the option to make some minor adjustments from my day-to-day shooting is kind of nice. Maybe it has to do with the stance that I am shooting in at the time. Being able to add spacers on the buttplate section would adjust the length of pull the rifle has and this may feel better while shooting in a prone position while I may want to remove them and get the rifle tucked in tighter for a standing unsupported position. In any matter, I like having the option of adjustment. Before fitting a buttplate on a stock, the stock should be cut and trued to accept whatever type of plate you are installing. Remember to give yourself a little bit more material than expected to allow room for adjustment during fitting. Fitting a flat buttplate is by far the easiest to do as it only requires that you mark the plates position on the stock, Mark your screw holes and secure the plate. Finally, use the marks made to the stock to shape the wood allowing for a clean looking finished product.

Some things can cost more to fix than they are worth.

For the purposes of this conversation, we will say a customer brings in a J.C. Higgins Model 20-gauge shotgun in poor condition with a split in the stock by the grip. This is no good as this is one of the places that needs to be the toughest, especially considering it is a shotgun. My options are to either repair it or replace it and I think we know what option is easier. However, I always leave the choosing to the client so they cannot say I chose the more expensive option so I could make more money off them.

Unfortunately, some things can cost more to fix than they are worth. Once I have determined the problem, I will usually look the make and model up on the Bluebook of Gun Values as I hold a subscription with them and use it regularly in my job as operations manager at the range I work at. They not only show up to date information on the current value of the firearm but the values history that shows any increases and decreases in value and when this occurred. After finding the guns' value I would begin to figure out what is needed to repair or replace the broken item and how much time it would take to finish the work. This helps me factor in the total cost of both the fix and the labor and then you add on the business profits margin and now you're ready to reach out to the customer.

Now armed with the knowledge of the issue, options to repair or replace the broken stuff, the cost of each option, and the value of the firearms being worked, you can begin talks with the client. Having a few different options and costs readily available for the customer is a professional way to approach any business transactions. Some people would pay anything to repair a family heirloom while others may see the cost as more than it's worth and call it quits but it is always best to let the client make that decision.

Repair and restoration of gunstock's.

Wood Preparation can be the key to a successful project and can mean the difference between an amazing looking finished product and a patchy piece of scrap wood. There are several things to consider when working on a gun stock. These can include Stain and oil, curing, return times, repointing the old checker patterns, the woods surface texture, and the surface sheen after you finished the project. So, let's begin to cover some of those things. When deciding what kind of look you want in the end you must first begin by making the decision to use a stain or just a rub on oil finish. If you're looking for a darker finish than the type of wood used can provide than add a stain but if you want to admire the beauty of a more natural look than just apply the oil as directed. Having said this, it's time to talk about curing and return times. Curing is critical in getting a well done, durable finish to your gun stock. Every product used to finish wood has different cure times that allow for the best results so do not rush this. Find out how long it takes for each step and return to it in the time instructed and you should have no issues.

On occasion someone with a gun stock that has already had checkering work done may need the existing design re-pointed. What this means is that the texture a checkering pattern may have had when it was new has worn down. This is the process of repairing individual diamonds or points. This not only improves the handling of the stock but brings back some of that appeal.

Choosing the wood's surface Texture and sheen are important as well and need to be considered throughout the entire process. So, what kind of checkering are you doing? Some examples include standard, borderless, skip a line, diamond and multi point checkering. Each serves their purpose so if you are looking for designs without borders or the elegant but still functional design of the classic diamond checkering then decide early and plan accordingly. Once the checkering is complete it is time to get the rifle to its final topcoat. Whether it is a matte finish or a high gloss, it's time to choose and apply the coat that best suits the desired results you want. Allow the proper cure times and you should be done.

SECTION SEVEN: OTHER CONSIDERATIONS

Three layperson, or "slang" terms used to communicate Common shooting malfunctions.

I feel it is important to talk to the customer and get as much information as possible before handling the firearm in question. This sounds easy but most of the time the customer has no idea what type of malfunction they are experiencing or even the name of the gun or part they think is broken. For example, if a firearm has a failure to feed the customer may come to you and say something like "I can't get the ammo in the gun" or "I racked it, and nothing happened." In my experience this is usually an operator error because the magazine was not seated correctly, or the slide was closed when they inserted the magazine, and they never pulled the slide back to chamber a round. Occasionally the magazine spring is under powered and actually is the cause of the malfunction. I would ask the customer if the magazine was left loaded for an extended period of time because this can damage the magazine spring and not feed ammunition correctly.

Now when the firearm has a failure to fire you may have the customer approach you and say things like "It did not work" or "I think its broken." My personal favorite was "Dis Choppa Don't Burn." I would usually start by asking what they are shooting so I can identify things like is there a safety and how does it work. A lot of times the customer has loaded the firearm correctly but forgot to disengage a safety selector switch or is not engaging the grip safety correctly. After I collect as much information as the customer has to offer, I can usually approach the firearm with a few ideas on how to fix the issue.

Finally, when the customer experiences a failure to extract, they may come to you and say things like "They keep getting stuck" or "My bullet will not come out." I usually ask if the firearm is jammed, and they respond with yes. At this point I ask if the ammo stuck in the barrel was fired or if it is still live. Once I have these answers, I'll have a better understanding of the issue and how to fix it. Making sure the firearm is clean and the extractor is not broken or missing I would clear the firearm, talk to the customer, and let them know why I think it happened. A lot of the malfunctions you come across are similar but be sure to take your time so as to avoid serious injury. It's easy to get complacent when this is your everyday work.

Explaining the differences between casting and swaging.

One of the main differences between casting and swaging is the tools used to complete the task. While casting bullets requires a method of melting metals, swagging doesn't need molten metal to create the round. This can be listed as an advantage for swagging because accident prone people may hurt themselves with sloppy pours. This also gives a point to swagging because you are much less likely to start a fire.

However, because you are filling a mold when casting bullets, you are much more likely to get the same bullet weight every time as opposed to swagging that can give you multiple bullet weights depending on how much material is added or even the types of material used. That is an advantage for casting being more consistent with regard to bullet weight.

This creates the challenge when swagging to create a number of bullets with consistent weights. Different bullet weights are obviously going to act differently when fired, even if the powder loads are identical. Heavier rounds fall faster than lighter ones and if someone makes their own ammunition for firing and wants to zero the optic that they have mounted on their firearm, they will have a difficult time using bullets that were swagged differently.

Explaining the difference between swaging with a reloading press and using a swaging press.

One of the biggest differences between swagging with a reloading press and using a swagging press is that the swagging press is specifically designed to do the job and the reloading press, though with the right attachments is capable of doing the job, is a tool meant for a different purpose. It would be like using a small flathead screwdriver as a punch. Yes, it may push the pin but because that was not its original design or purpose, something was just damaged or broken.

An advantage I see with using a reloading press with dies meant for swagging is that the one tool has just become two. Another would be that I am saving money not having to purchase the second tool, the swagging press. The disadvantage would be that a tool used twice as much, wears out in half the time compared to one that was kept to its original intent.

I feel like it is really important to use the right tool for the job in any case. I believe anyone who has spent a number of years doing this professionally will admit that in a pinch you find what gets the job done and you move on to the next task. Though this may or may not be the case, everyone knows that the right tool always makes the task ten times easier.

I believe the who would pick what option is really dependent on the type of person is looking to get into this. If you are the type of person who wants benchrest quality bullets, then you are also probably the type of person who would buy the right equipment to do so. But if you just want reasonable quality bullets and are working on a budget, you also might be the person to buy the R suffix dies and repurpose your reloading press to get the job done.

Considering different source materials for casting bullets.

There are a ton of options for procuring lead, tin, and antimony for casting your own bullets. With a quick google search one of the first options available is on Amazon. It gives you the option to buy 10lbs of bullet casting alloy for $59.99. It comes in ingot and is cleaned and ready to melt and cast. Another option would be to reclaim the alloy from your local firing range. This is a free and easy option if you work at a range as I do but comes at its own cost still. Anyone who has worked at a range can tell you that the berm, especially rubber berms, will fill up and become dangerous if not cleaned out on occasion. This can be a physically daunting task but allows you to reclaim the alloys free of cost. However, this is not a clean option and will require separating lead from copper jackets and steel core ammunition that had been fired. Also, it includes the cost of the propane used in the crucible to melt the metals and clean out the junk that is not ready to use alloy.

If the user of these metals is only doing a small batch of hand loads than I can see either option as a cost-effective option but if attempting to fill a huge order for a client needing bullets than the actual cost and time needed to achieve this may be too high for some. Nevertheless, being able to cast your own bullets is an extremely valuable skill to have because the market for ammunition can be volatile at times. Every election season or second amendment scare to hit the market creates a run-on ammunition as well as firearms. When this happens things like bullets and primers become hard to find and increasingly expensive. That is when it really may become the cheaper option to cast your own bullets.

The construction, materials, and use of a frangible bullet.

Frangible ammunition can be used for a number of different reasons, but most revolve around the point of safe training. Used by many different militaries around the world for CQB training, frangible ammunition is designed to fragment on impact with a hard target like steel or concrete. Most of this type of ammunition is made up of copper alloy and a composite of sorts mixed with a bonding agent and pressed to shape with a high-pressure method. This is to ensure that the projectile stays together while being fired through the barrel of the firearm but upon impact will pulverize into safer tiny fragments and reduce the risk of ricochet and injury.

The advantages of using this type of ammunition are listed by my classmates and made finding a different one very difficult. After reviewing an NRA website on the topic, I realized that one of the coolest advantages of this type of ammunition is that it is most often made of nontoxic materials unlike traditional ammunition made with lead that can be toxic if exposed to. This is amazing because the use of traditional ammunition outdoors will embed lead toxins into the berms, and this can leach into the ground and eventually contaminate things like well water on the property.

Probably one of the biggest disadvantages of this type of training ammunition is that most people hear "training ammunition" and think it is less lethal or non-lethal ammunition. The fact that most people have never heard of this type of ammunition means a lack of knowledge and a risk of misuse. If fired at another individual the user risks causing serious injury and or death to the individual fired at. If this type of ammunition hits an individual and fragments inside of them the risk of injury and or death is increased because unlike traditional ammunition that wants to pernitrate, frangible ammunition may break apart inside and damage multiple vital organs. Please be sure that anyone using frangible ammunition knows the risk involved and you should be able to reduce the risk of injury.

Questions you can ask the customer to rule out operator error or bad ammunition.

With regard to the ammunition and whether or not it is the issue there are a few ways to determine the problem. First, I would ask the customer where they got the ammunition and how it was stored. This tells me if they bought it from the factory or if it has passed hands a few times before being fired. It also tells me if moisture has gotten to the ammunition causing it not to fire. It may be factory ammunition and they may store it correctly but if not bought from a reputable dealer but rather some guy at a show there is no guarantee that the previous owner stored the ammunition in a way that damaged it or not. Operator error is a different beast in itself. You may need to play twenty questions with someone to determine the actual issue because there are so many ways the user of the firearm may have attempted to use it incorrectly. It sounds silly but if someone tells me their firearm isn't firing one of the first questions, I have for them is did they chamber a round. It is too often someone will insert a magazine on a closed slide or action, and they tried to fire without chambering a round first. The very next questions I have are usually does their firearm have a safety, what kind, and did they disengage it. Sometimes the customer is so new to the firearm they cannot answer something as basic as this and that is okay. Remember, Ignorance is curable if you take the time to teach others what they may be doing wrong.

Potential ramifications a customer may face by having the trigger of a firearm modified.

Once the firearms action is modified beyond its factory specifications the individual who commissioned the work and possibly the gunsmith who did the work may see legal ramifications because the prosecutor may label this firearm unsafe or dangerous now. Now if the individual owner of the firearm decided to do the work themselves and are not armorer level certified to do so, it is possible that the individual sees legal issues for manufacturing a firearm without a license. If the individual who commissioned the work claims the firearm was modified more than what was commissioned and attempts to blame the gunsmith for an accidental shooting, the gunsmith then can become entangled in the legal mess that follows.

One potential ramification a gunsmith or armorer might face when modifying the trigger of a customer's firearm.

When a crime or accidental shooting occurs the responding agency may seize the firearm and take a close look at things like the ammunition used or any aftermarket modifications that were done. It is possible that the individual's attorney advises their client to push the blame on the gunsmith who performed the work on the firearm in an attempt to clear their client of any wrongdoing. It is one thing to drop a 10Lb trigger to normal 3Lb – 6Lb trigger but when a gunsmith performs a job that drops the trigger to a dangerous 1Lb pull then they may be asking for real trouble.

One strategy practicing gunsmiths and armorers use to protect themselves and why that strategy is something you would use in your shop.

I believe it is smart for any gunsmith to have clients sign waivers that indemnify the gunsmith of any and all responsibility for wrong doings with the firearm after the work is completed. This legal document is all the gunsmiths will need to present to the courts to clear them of any liability. This strategy is absolutely something we do at the current facility I work at and will be something I continue to do when I open my own shop in the future.

Making the argument that piston-driven systems are better platforms for gas-operated weapons.

So, I have chosen to use Gun Digest as my gun publication of choice, and I will be arguing the point that piston driven firearms are better than direct gas impingement. While the article does list facts in favor of both types of firearms, the first two examples, they list are in favor of the gas piston operation. First, they say "Piston-driven guns run much cleaner" and I can agree with this statement. Most of the carbon buildup happens in the tube that the piston sits in and never reaches the action or bolt assembly making it run more reliably. A number of militaries around the world run piston driven firearms for this reason. When you need your machine gun to run and your life depends on it, this seems like the right choice.

Second, they say "Piston-driven guns run much cooler" and again I will have to agree with them on this. If firing a few rounds at a time with both types of firearms, you may not realize a difference but with a sustained rate of fire the difference is noticeable. Also, speaking from experience I have seen the direct gas impingement of the AR platform fail when running full auto for too long. The gas tube can get to a glowing red-hot state and on rare occasions the tube splits and out gases instead of directing the gas needed to continue cycling the bolt. Granted this was during a torture test but to prove this I ran four thirty round magazines through a full auto M-16 and was able to light my cigarette off the gas tube. Seems a little too hot and unreliable to me.

Common features of most of the firearms in Henry's Firearms guide.

The Henry rifle company has been around for a long time and was patented back in 1860. Most of their models use the iconic leaver action to feed, chamber, extract and eject ammunition and have done so since their earliest model. Some of the models we are going to discuss today have very different and unique features but while looking at all the models listed in the Henry user manual, I could only find one feature that every rifle has in common and that is the inclusion of iron sights. While most models give you the option to attach a sight, all of them come with iron sights as a standard.

So, let us begin to discuss some of Henrys different models and features that make them stand out amongst the others. To start, let's go over Henrys drastically different rifle type, the AR-7 also known as their survival rifle. This is their only model of rifle that uses a detachable magazine that can be stored in the butt stock. Its most unique feature is its ability to be taken down to pieces and stored in its butt stock along with its magazine. Most takedown rifles fold or come apart but the AR-7 is one of the only makes and models that stores completely in its stock. Next, we have Henrys Mini Bolt H005 Series Rifle designed for youth shooting. This is their only bolt action rifle listed in the user manual and does not have any type of magazine or feeding device. Henry's unique feature here is that the user places a single round in the chamber and then locks it in the barrel using its bolt. Usually with most bolt action rifles you are ready to fire at this point. However, Henry has another unique feature on their Mini Bolt H005 that requires the shooter to pull back on the cocking mechanism before it will fire.

Henry does offer a pump action model rifle with the octagon barrel known as the H0003T. This model is unique because it uses the tube fed option seen on most Henry Leaver actions but operates like a pump action shotgun. Switching to the topic of Henry's leaver action rifle types, I realized that most of their leaver action models do not have safety selector switches.

However, some models like the 30-30 and 45-70 have Henry's "ultra-safe patented Transfer Bar Safety Mechanism." This is not a standard selector switch like what is found on most rifles today but rather a unique failsafe design that blocks the firing mechanism if the hammer falls for any other reason other than pulling the trigger. Other henry rifles are designed with a "safe" position to cock the hammer. It can be set this way from the cocked position or the closed firing position. Some people call this the quarter cocked position, and it can be found on some single action revolvers as well. Henry has been making some amazing rifles for a long time now, proving that an oldie can indeed still be a goodie.

Conducting outside research into an option to purchase a "mini lathe."

First, describe the lathe you reviewed. Discuss its capabilities, set up, and cost.

The metal lathe I chose to review is the Eastwood Benchtop Mini Metal Lathe—7 Inch x 12 Inch. As it mentions, this is a benchtop lathe capable of cutting different metals and has a 7inch x 12inch working area. This unit cost about $1,018.99 and has many features and some amazing reviews. To start, it is a manageable size to fit most home workshops. It also comes with both inside and outside three jaw chuck sets and a few HSS cutting tools. Setup is also quite easy compared to full size metal lathes. Just find a lever surface and mount your base, clean and oil the working parts, check calibration and off you go. Finally, it has an Auto-feed and selectable gear train component used for precision cutting and threading work and its 3/4HP motor plugs it into a 120-volt power current avoiding the need to rewire the outlet of your workspace.

Based on the types of jobs you would perform with it, a "mini lathe" is a good investment, but I would rather "farm out" machine work to a dedicated shop and here is why.

Now this will be hard for me to say because I hate asking others for help and if possible, I would always rather do the work myself, but I think I would probably go the route of "farming out" the machine work with a dedicated machine shop. It's not that I don't want to spend the money because this is cheap considering its capabilities and it's not like I don't want to learn the machine because I already have a working knowledge of the lathe. I do see purchasing a lathe for your shop as a good investment but for me what it boils down to is usable space and the frequency at which I would end up using this machine. Because I do not own a space with a ton of counter space and taking into consideration that this machine should be mounted in place for operation, I don't think I can sacrifice that amount of space for a machine I don't think I would need very often.

The procedure for setting up a Grizzly Industries heavy duty drill press, per the owner's manual.

The heavy-duty drill press I have chosen for the purpose of this conversation is the Grizzly Industries heavy duty drill press G0751. When looking at some of the other models of drill press Grizzly Industries offers, I noticed in the customer reviews posted to The Home Depot website that customers rate the other machines lower claiming they are a little ridged because they were made in China. I was able to find the owner's manual for this specific machine on a website called ManualsLib.com. This was a great resource and allowed me to read all about the machine before deciding to purchase one. The Home Depot only had one review for this drill press, but they gave it a 5-star rating and said it worked well.

The procedure for setting up the press, per the owner's manual.

Well, the machine uses power to operate so one of the first things the owner's manual talks about is the voltage required and how to ground it properly to avoid the risk of fire. It then goes on to give the end user unpacking instructions for what might be needed to set it up and the manual includes an inventory of parts that should come with the machine. After the cleaning and degreasing instructions, the manual lists site considerations for the safest placement that offers optimal performance.

Describing the steps you need to take to calibrate the press, and what components you should check for wear.

When calibrating the drill press you can start on page 42 where it talks about adjusting your Gibs and lead screw backlash. On pages 43 and 44 of the owner's manual it talks about calibrating and adjusting the tramming spindle to be sure your drill press is properly aligned. On page 45 it talks about adjusting your return spring tension and beyond that it won't speak tons on calibration. There is a lengthy section that covers trouble shooting but not a ton on calibration or common wear spots.

Describing one accessory you might wish to add to your set up, and how it would benefit your operation.

I like all the features this grizzly drill press has already. However, the working surface and the base where the coolant is being recycled and pumped have a decent amount of space between them. This leads me to believe that as I pump the coolant onto my work surface, it may splash away from the base meaning every time it is used there will be a degree of waist and mess because of this. I may decide to find or create a splash guard to better recycle the coolant fluid.

Is the finish that was used on your H&K VP9 a good option for its purpose? Why or why not?

I have carried this pistol for years for self-defense purposes and only ever had to draw it once when living in Baltimore Maryland to defend another person in a tough spot. Thankfully, I did not need to use it that day, but I was confident it was going to work when I needed it.

The finish on the slide is a surface conversion coating and is very durable. I have carried this in a Kydex OWB holster for years and this would usually work down a surface coat type of finish pretty fast. Even the bake on finish of the Cerakote job used on my Taurus Judge wore down much faster than this conversion coating. The slide does show some dents and dings to the finish closer to the muzzle but all in all it has held up great over the years. Used for indoor and outdoor training its rust resistant coating has held up great and having practiced drawing from a holster thousands of times I am still amazed at how well it still looks. I believe it is the best finish for the firearms intended purpose because it is exposed to the elements every day and holds up great.

Touch up work using Cerakote can be achieved with the use of an experienced technician but if done by an inexperienced individual you can run into a bunch of issues. The color doesn't match, spray on finish was too thick or shows evidence of running or dripping. Just talk to your local Cerakote specialist about your firearm and your options for touch up work and you may be surprised at their answer. However, touch up work on the H&K VP9 Slide is going to be a little more difficult. You could use some perma-blue on bare metal sections, but this is a different process than the original conversion coating.

H&K calls their slide coating their Hostile Environment finish which is just a cool marketing term for a really great finish. In fact, the way they finish their slides is through a process called Melanite Nitriding that enriches the metal with nitrogen and carbon. This technique gives a deep finish that also increases the density of the metal making it pretty difficult to be work down. Even with daily carry of the firearm and the abuse it takes while conducting training, the slides finish is not easily damaged or worn and this can be directly attributed to the type of finish they apply as a factory standard. An alternative finish would only take an already great finish and turn it into one that breaks down faster. If I had damaged the finish that bad, I would investigate having the Melanite Nitriding redone because in my experience it is one of the most durable finish available.

My final thoughts on the shooting sports business and gunsmithing in general.

There is a lot more to gunsmithing than just working on firearms if you intend to start your own business doing so. This book covered everything from the licensing needed for federal, state, and local jurisdictions to putting in the work needed to successfully manage and run a shooting sports business. Most of the contents of this book are opinion based but were written with both research and personal knowledge backing them. Believe it or not, this book and its contents barely scratch the surface of the never-ending work of a good gunsmith, so I encourage others to continue their education and further their knowledge of such topics.

It is and always will be important for anyone handling a firearm to keep a focus on safety. The author of this book and its publisher are not responsible for any injury sustained by someone who mishandled a firearm as a result of trying anything talked about throughout the book. I will always preach safety to both my students and my readers because there are some mistakes you cannot come back from in this business. Additionally, the author and its publisher are not responsible for any damage caused to a firearm as a result of someone attempting to alter the firearm from its original state. In other words, please don't send hate mail because you messed up your Hydro Dip project.

You will get out of this business only what you put in so remember that if you are starting your own company from scratch, read, and reread this book and be prepared to put in some long hours. Simply knowing the things discussed in this book will not guarantee you will have a successful business. It will take time and a lot of hard work to succeed in this industry. Put in the work and earn a good living!

SOURCE MATERIAL

Business licenses and permits that are required to open/start up a firearms business in my area.

https://gov.texas.gov/uploads/files/business/Texas_Licenses_Permits_Guide.pdf

The requirements for importing the firearms your business wants to import.

"Bureau of Alcohol, Tobacco, Firearms and Explosives." Firearms—Guides—Importation & Verification of Firearms, Ammunition and Implements of War—Types of Importers | Bureau of Alcohol, Tobacco, Firearms and Explosives, www.atf.gov/firearms/firearms-guides-importation-verification-firearms-ammunition-and-implements-war-types. Accessed 31 May 2023.

Two variants of blow back operation type handguns.

https://firearmsguide.com/index.php?option=com_firearms&view=firearms&Itemid=106.

The Purpose of a Choke and the Installation Procedure for a Ventilated Rib.

https://www.youtube.com/watch?v=ygC6mrpVz74

http://addaribs.com/products_info.htm

"Shotgun Choke Tube Information." Shotgun Choke Information, https://trulockchokes.com/basic_choke_information.html.

Author Nathan Fosters prescribed methods to remove the rifle as a variable.

Foster, Nathan. The Practical Guide to Bolt Action Rifle Accurizing and Maintenance. Terminal Ballistics Research, 2014.

When Bedding a Rifle, should you free-float the entire barrel?

Foster, Nathan. The Practical Guide to Bolt Action Rifle Accurizing and Maintenance. Terminal Ballistics Research, 2014.

https://gundigest.com/rifles/barrel-bedding-affect-accuracy

What Is Rifle Bedding?, https://www.ballisticstudies.com/Knowledgebase/What+is+rifle+bedding.html

Interesting aftermarket work that can be performed on a 1911 firearm.

"Accuracy x R1 Open Race Gun 2011." TK Custom Store, tkcustom.com/products/accuracy-x-r1-open-racegun-2011. Accessed 31 May 2023.

A customer requested you service his favorite family heirloom—a World War II Arisaka Type 2.

Nambu World: Arisaka Type 2 Paratroop Rifle

Discussing the definition of what makes a rifle accurate and what makes it inaccurate.

"Basic Rifle Accuracy and Ballistics." Terminal Ballistics Research. www.Ballisticstudies.com/knowledgebase/ Basic+Rifle+Accuracy+And+Ballistics.HTML

Considering different source materials for casting bullets.

Bullet Casting Alloy (10lb Ingot—Amazon.com. https://www.amazon. com/Bullet-Casting-Alloy-10lb-Ingot/dp/B01F5SBBXQ.

The construction, materials, and use of a frangible bullet.

https://www.nrafamily.org/content/ frangible-ammunition-pros-cons-myths

Potential ramifications a customer may face by having the trigger of a firearm modified.

USCCA, and Thomas Kral. "Bland, Basic, Boring and Black." Alpha Koncepts, 3 Nov. 2019, https://www.alphakoncepts.com/blog/ bland-basic-boring-and-black/.

Making the argument that piston-driven systems are better platforms for gas-operated weapons.

Mann, Richard A. "6 Facts about AR-15 Direct Impingement vs. Gas Piston." Gun Digest, 21 May 2020, https://gundigest.com/gun-reviews/ rifles-reviews/ar-15-gas-impingement-vs-piston.

Common features of most of the firearms in Henry's Firearms guide.

https://moodle-content.s3.amazonaws.com/ FTT+Textbooks/2021+Updates/NonSDI/Henry+Guide.pdf

Conducting outside research into an option to purchase a "mini lathe."

Eastwood benchtop mini metal lathe—7-inch x 12 inch. Retrieved March 15, 2023, from https://www.eastwood.com/eastwood-mini-lathe.html?gclid=Cj0KCQjw2cWgBhDYARIsALggUho1LPL8STq_w2eBHKfCkKRE1rmnzn-egTqXXE3M0FC-YeusUnhbFzgaAqerEALw_wcB&wcid=18669317250&wickedid=629883587211&wickedsource=google&wv=4

The procedure for setting up a Grizzly Industries heavy duty drill press, per the owner's manual.

https://www.homedepot.com/p/Grizzly-Industrial-Heavy-Duty-Drill-Press-G0751/310230036

"Grizzly G0751 Owner's Manual PDF Download." Manuals Lib, 4 Dec. 2013, https://www.manualslib.com/manual/564610/Grizzly-G0751.html#manual.

The science and definitions of both velocity and speed

https://www.britannica.com/technology/ballistic-pendulum

The Physical Science that applies when firing a bullet

Shipman, James. An Introduction to Physical Science. Available from: VitalSource Bookshelf, (15th Edition). Cengage Learning US, 2020.

The Concept of Chemistry Relates to Gunpowder and Primers

"Askrose.Org Types of Bonds and Their Differences—Chemistry—Bonding and Molecular Structure:AskRose." AskRose.Org, 20 July 2020, askrose.org/student-resources/science-resources/chemistry/bonding-and-molecularstructure/typesofbondsandtheirdifferences/#:~:text=The%20difference%20between%20bond%20types,don't%20share%20at%20all.

Choosing a type of wood for a custom stock build

Sonoran Desert Institute. "Wood for Gunstocks." *Customizing & Woodworking*, Sonoran Desert Institute, 2021, page 7-12

Critical measurements when custom making a gun stock.

Sonoran Desert Institute. "Wood for Gunstocks." *Customizing & Woodworking*, Sonoran Desert Institute, 2021, pages 31-33

Considering options to reduce felt recoil.

Maddox, Brandon. "Which Gun Has the Most Recoil?" *Silencer Central*, 10 May 2023, www.silencercentral.com/blog/which-gun-has-the-most-recoil/#:~:text=The%20correct%20answer%20to%20what,caliber%20probably%20takes%20the%20cake.